BY THE EDITORS OF
CONSUMER GUIDE®

Patchwork Quilts

BEEKMAN HOUSE
New York

Broken Star ∧ pg. 11, ∨ **12**

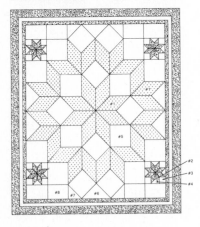

Manufactured in the United States of America.
10 9 8 7 6 5 4 3 2 1

Library of Congress Catalog Card Number:
82-62230
ISBN: 0-517-381168

This edition published by:
Beekman House
Distributed by Crown Publishers, Inc.
One Park Avenue
New York, New York 10016

CREDITS

Quilt patterns and photographs courtesy Lady's Circle Editor's Choice Patchwork Quilts, Lopez Publications, Inc.
Editorial Director: Carter Houck
Photography: Myron Miller

Cover Design: Frank E. Peiler

Note: When patterns are not included, it is due to the fact that these are personalized designs and belong to the makers of the quilts. We have no pattern service and cannot supply any designs other than those given in this book.

Contents

Quilting: A Craft That Takes Tradition Into The Twenty-First Century

People who can't bear to throw anything away justify their desire to "hoard" on the grounds that fashion goes in cycles and everything comes back into style sooner or later. And, they point out, today's white elephant may well be tomorrow's heirloom.

Quilting is perfect proof of the truth of both arguments. The warmth and comfort of quilts and the easy-going effect that patchwork gives a room are just right for today's relaxed living styles. And quilted work ages beautifully. Many gorgeous spreads, throws, pillows—even pictures—lovingly quilted generations ago have become family treasures in American homes.

One of the most attractive aspects of quilting is its versatility. Because it's based on the simple premise of putting together small pieces of fabric to form a design, you can use up all the odds and ends you've stashed away from years of sewing. Or pick up bargain-priced remnants from the fabric store. You can recycle fabrics, ribbons, and laces from out-of-fashion or out-grown clothing. You can get each of your friends and neighbors to contribute a favorite scrap of material and put them all together to make a friendship quilt—what nicer way to remember the people you love or to create a memento of a certain time of your life? The giver's embroidered autograph on each patch makes your work even more special.

Quilting is a social craft; the tradition was established by groups of quilters who met together to create one beautiful quilt. You can still quilt in a group; you can do it while you talk to your friends; you can even quilt while you watch television. It's a creative form of needlework, with the possibilities limited only by your own imagination. And—best of all—it's not difficult to do.

This book is designed to have something for everyone—from beginner to expert. As long as you understand the basics of quilting, there's a pattern for you here. Along with full-size pattern pieces, you'll find to-scale piecing diagrams to help you put the design together. The "expert" patterns at the beginning of the book are for experienced quilters; these are followed by "intermediate" designs for quilters who've gotten beyond the beginner stage but still feel challenged. The final section is for the "beginner" who's still in the early stages of mastering this intriguing form of handwork.

Apart from making spreads and throws, you can use these detailed patterns and clear instructions to quilt a lovely hoop-framed picture for your wall, or a stunning patchwork bolero worked in silk and velvet after the European style.

Among the styles that will appeal to the beginner is a Victorian design that uses dozens of different colors to form squares within squares to give a most sophisticated effect. But it's easy because you're working only with squares and triangles. This is one for the beginner with lots of imagination—as with so much of the best patchwork, it's the contrast and balance of colors that makes for individuality. Another way to experiment with contrast is to marry different types of fabrics—like the silk and velvet used to give the luxury look to the bolero mentioned earlier. This piece is further embellished with embroidery and crewel work.

One of the delights of quilting is recreating something beautiful from the past. Another beginner's pattern included in this book lets you try 19th century quilts from Maine that use brick and triangle shapes to create the bold, zig-zag Lightning design. For more advanced quilters there's a quilt called New York Beauty, made by Edna Herston of Arizona who finished it in 1855; her great-grandson later presented it to the Arizona Museum. It's an elaborate design worked in white with red, yellow, and green to reflect the strong, bright colors of the quilter's home state. But you could design a striking alternative color scheme with muted shades.

Apart from the quilts for which patterns are given, there are others to whet your imagination and make your fingers itch to take on greater challenges. Like the Tree Of Life, worked in decorator fabrics to simulate the Palampore quilts of the 18th century. Or a finely detailed Scandinavian Peasant Quilt. Or perhaps you could duplicate the intricate Star Of Bethlehem quilt made in 1850 and now displayed at the Dewitt Historical Society in Ithaca. Even more exotic are two wonderful examples of Victorian silk and velvet throws, both elaborately hand-embroidered and both exceptional tributes to the creativity and craftsmanship of their designers.

Whatever your level of ability, this book is designed to help you enjoy and appreciate even more both the historical background to this form of needlework and the pleasure that it can give you today. The patterns are exciting, and carefully geared to different skill levels. The pattern pieces are full-size, and the directions are clear and easy-to-follow. And remember that even if you're a beginner—you won't be a beginner forever. Start slowly and work your way up through patterns of increasing complexity and maybe you, too, will have the pleasure of creating a 20th century work that will be treasured by your family generations from now.

Cochise County

The blocks are 20 inches square. Each block is surrounded with a 1-inch red band and set with 1-inch blue-green sashes and a 3-inch border in the same color. The binding is red. The neat Clamshell quilting adds interest to the white background spaces.

For each block cut:
- 1 yellow #1
- 4 red #2
- 4 blue-green #2
- 4 yellow #3
- 16 red #4
- 4 blue-green #5

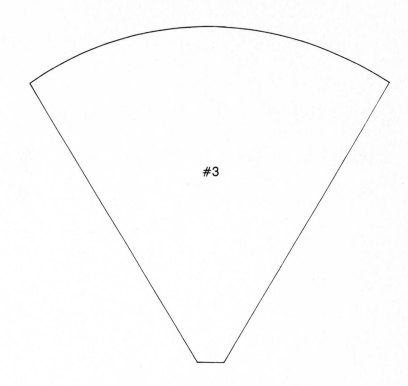

One-fourth size pattern.

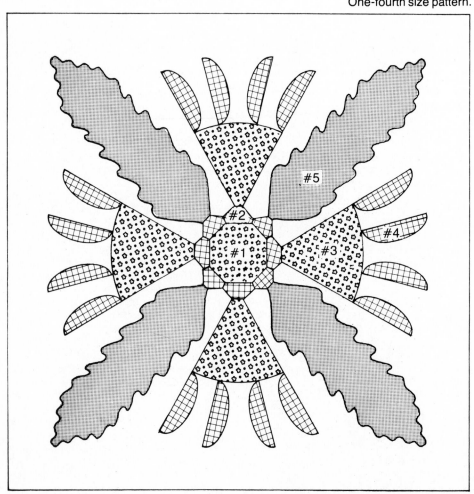

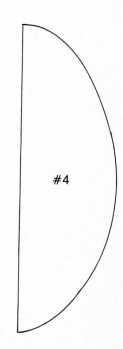

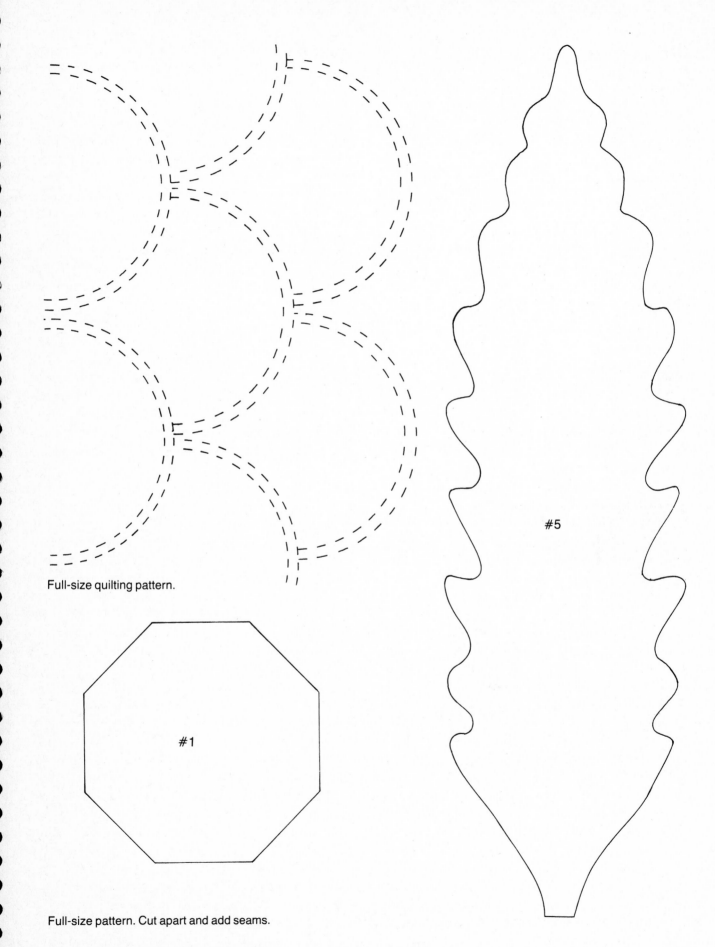

Full-size quilting pattern.

#5

#1

Full-size pattern. Cut apart and add seams.

5

Wiscasset Quilts

These handsomely pieced, appliquéd quilts from the 1930's are made in colors that are nearly impossible to repeat today. The muslin backgrounds have a softening effect—but the pure cotton fabrics themselves are in exceptionally muted shades.

On both designs it is wise to piece as much of the center and corner block motifs as possible, then appliqué the rest in place. The sets and borders seem such an integral part of the original designs that it might be better to leave them as is—we don't suggest redesigning other than by doing your own color blending.

Blue Quilt

For each block cut:
  1 muslin 22-inch square, add seams
  1 each #1 through #3
  4 each #4 through #7

For sashes cut:
  2 strips 22 inches by 1½ inches wide, add seams
  2 each #8 through #10

For first border cut:
  2 strips 1½ inches wide, add seams
  1 strip, ¾ inch wide, add seams
  Additional #8 through #10

For outer borders cut:
  4 strips, ¾ to 1¾ inches wide, add seams

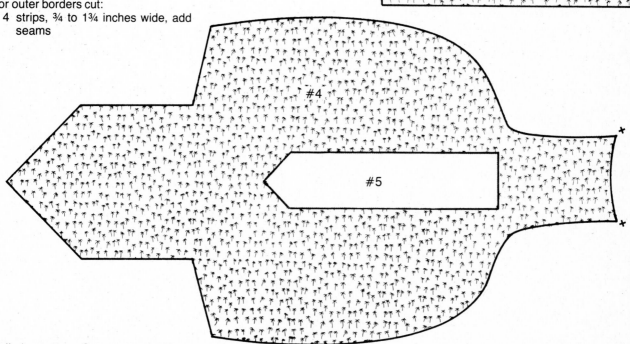

Full-size pattern. Cut apart and add seams.

6

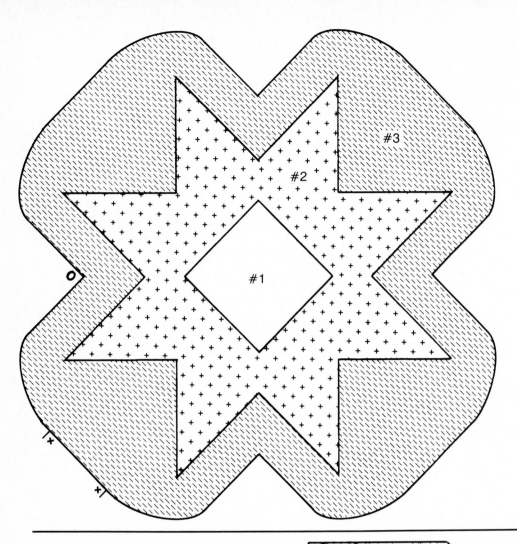

Full-size corner block for green quilt.
Cut apart and add seams.

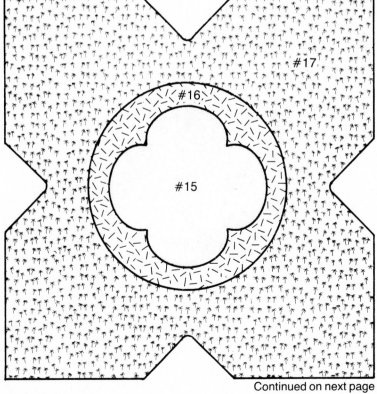

Continued on next page

Wiscasset Quilts

Green Quilt

For each block cut:
    1 muslin 22-inch square, add seams
    1 each #1 through #3
    8 solid #4
    4 each #5 through #14

For sashes cut:
    2 strips 22 inches by 1½ inches
       wide, add seams
    2 each #15 through #17

For first border cut:
    1 strip 1½ inches wide, add seams
    Additional #15 through #17

For outer borders cut:
    2 strips 1¼ inches wide, add seams

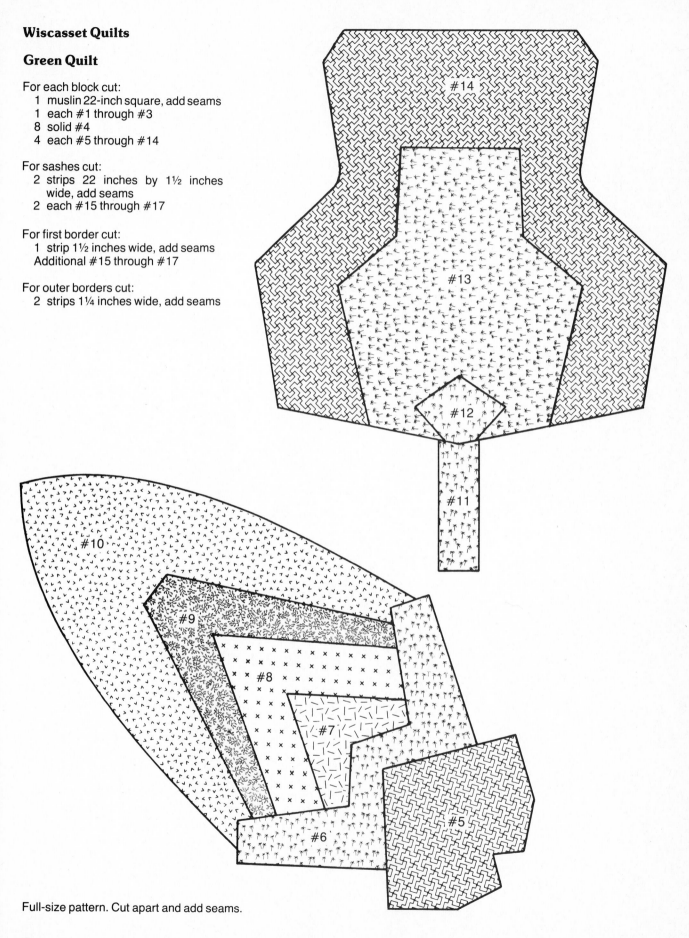

Full-size pattern. Cut apart and add seams.

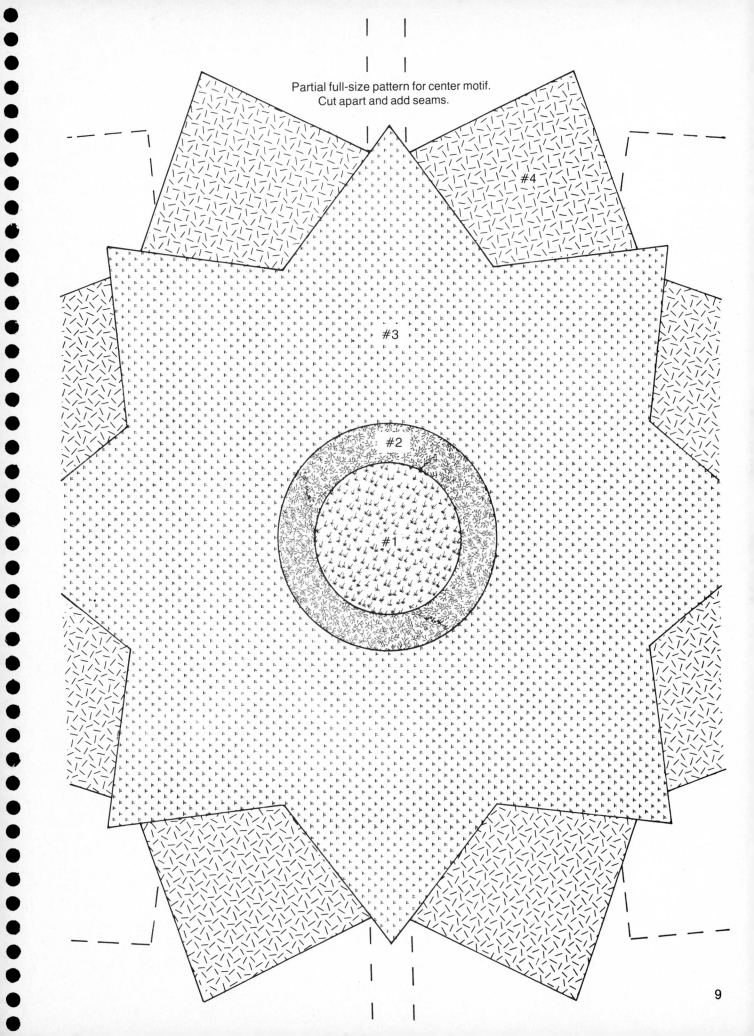

Partial full-size pattern for center motif.
Cut apart and add seams.

#4

#3

#2

#1

9

Little Giant

The hands of an expert make this design look a lot easier than it is.

Each large block is framed with a dark border, ¾ inch wide. The print sashes and outer dark border are 3 inches wide and the binding is of the print. Four blocks across and five in length make a nice large quilt. The quilting is outline and diagonal filler.

For each 15½-inch block cut:
- 1 dark #1
- 4 dark #2
- 4 print #2
- 4 white #3
- 4 white #3A
- 8 white #4
- 4 white #5
- 8 print #5
- 4 white #6
- 4 dark #6
- 4 white #7
- 4 white #7A
- 4 dark #8
- 4 dark #8A

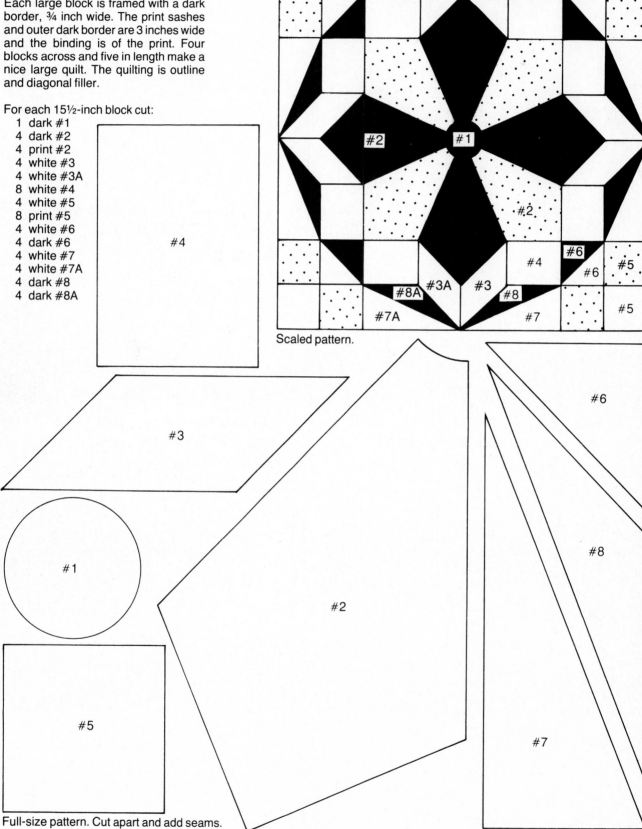

Scaled pattern.

Full-size pattern. Cut apart and add seams.

10

Broken Star

Catherine Dyer of Danvers, Massachusetts, used diChesere templates (slightly less than 2-inch diamonds) and her "spare time" to make her full-bed Broken Star in five months. Good trick since she did it all by hand and works a regular five-day week besides. She credits her husband's helpful support for at least part of that success. It is shown here in the 17th-century Claflin-Richards House in Wenham, which is now open as a museum. Expert.
King-size pattern on page 12

Broken Star

The six colors of Catherine's Broken Star blend together for an almost antique effect in a design that is often seen in bright bold colors in other parts of the country. Each diamond point is arranged in the same gradation, using the #1 diamond pieces. The smaller corner stars are made of only three colors.

For each #1 star point section cut the following #1 diamonds:
    6 dark green (A)
    10 green print (B)
    8 pink (C)
    6 light print (D)
    4 green (E)
    2 medium green (F)

For each #2 star point section cut the following #2 diamonds:
    2 dark green (G)

    1 pink (H)
    1 medium green print (I)

    4 each white #3 and #4
    20 white #5 12-inch squares, add seams
    6 white #6 12-inch right-angle triangles, add seams
    4 white #7 8½-inch right-angle triangles, add seams
    8 white #8 8½ by 12 inches, add seams

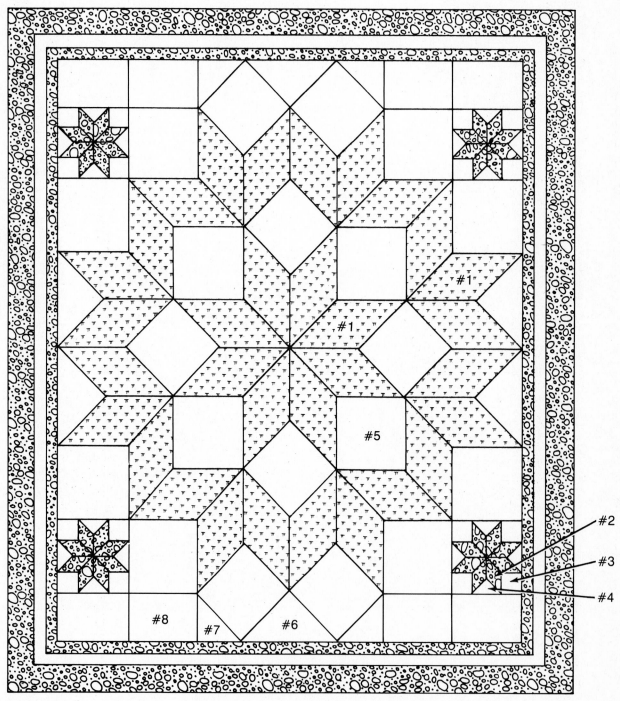

Scaled pattern of entire 98- × 116-inch quilt.

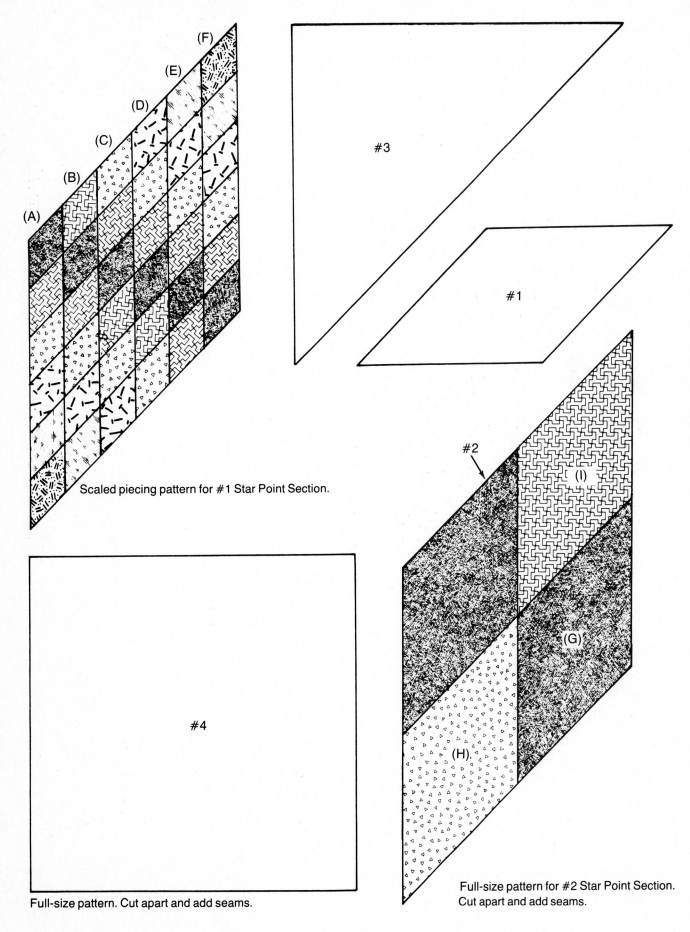

(F)
(E)
(D)
(C)
(B)
(A)

#3

#1

Scaled piecing pattern for #1 Star Point Section.

#2

(I)

(G)

(H)

#4

Full-size pattern. Cut apart and add seams.

Full-size pattern for #2 Star Point Section.
Cut apart and add seams.

Feathered Star

Only the expert should tackle any Feathered Star—this one especially. You will find the usual geometric inaccuracy in the straight and slanted rows of "feathers" or small #6 triangles. It takes a little cheating in the stitching to make them work.

For each 25-inch block cut:
    1 red #1
    4 muslin #1
    8 red #2
    8 muslin #2
    8 green #3
    4 red #4
    8 green #5
  72 muslin #6
  60 red #6
    4 muslin #7, 8¼-inch right-angle triangle, add seams
    4 muslin #8, 6¾-inch square, add seams

For sashes cut:
    red diamonds #9
    green triangles #10

For 8-inch muslin border cut:
    red bows #11
    green swags #12
    (appliquéd swags can be lengthened or shortened on fold line)

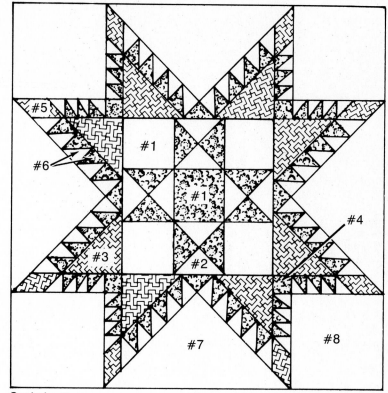

Scaled pattern.

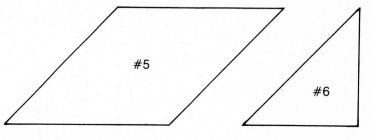

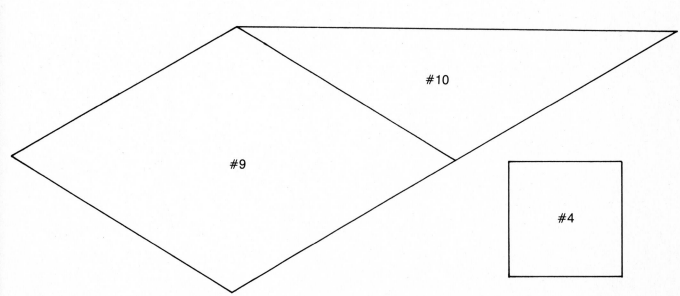

Full-size pattern. Cut apart and add seams.

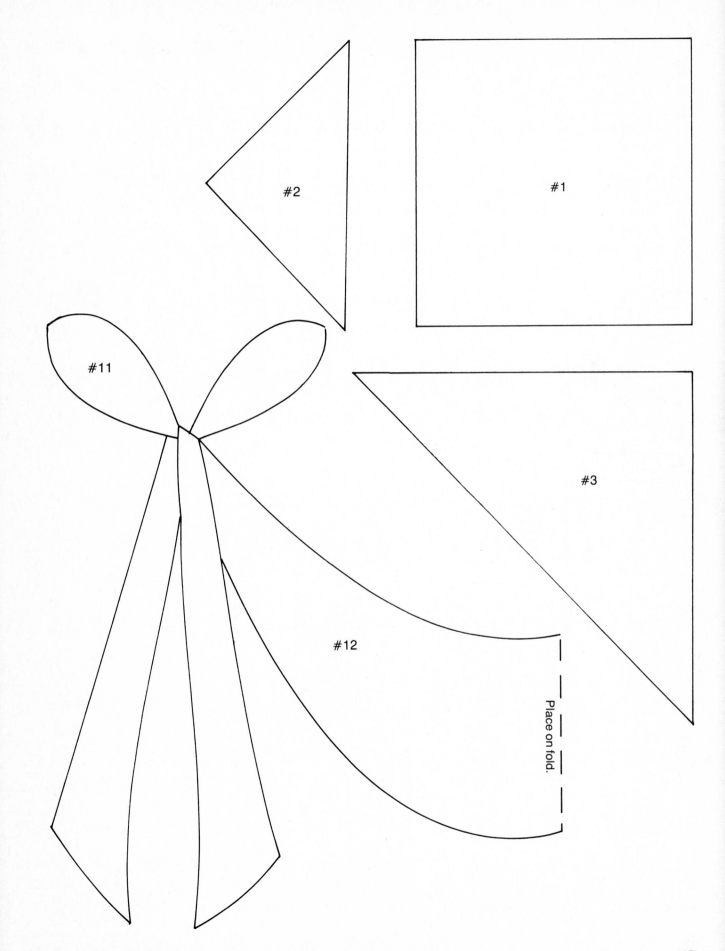

#2

#1

#11

#3

#12

Place on fold.

15

Fish Circle

Made up in this octagon shape, a Star design will not only fit well into a hoop frame but can be pieced into a quilt with squares set between. (Work it out on paper first.)

For each 20-inch octagon cut:
- 2 dark #1
- 2 medium #1
- 2 light #1
- 2 solid #1
- 8 white #2
- 4 dark #3
- 4 medium #3
- 4 light #3
- 4 solid #3
- 8 white #4
- 8 white #5

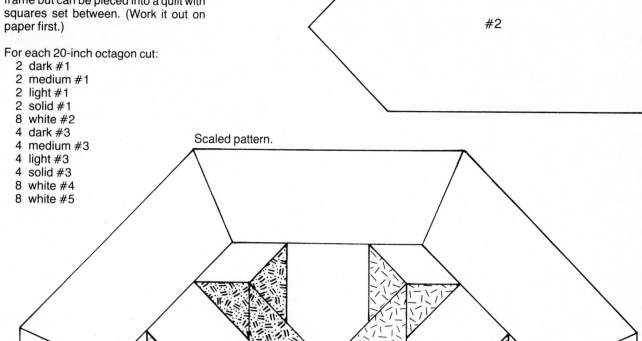

#2

Scaled pattern.

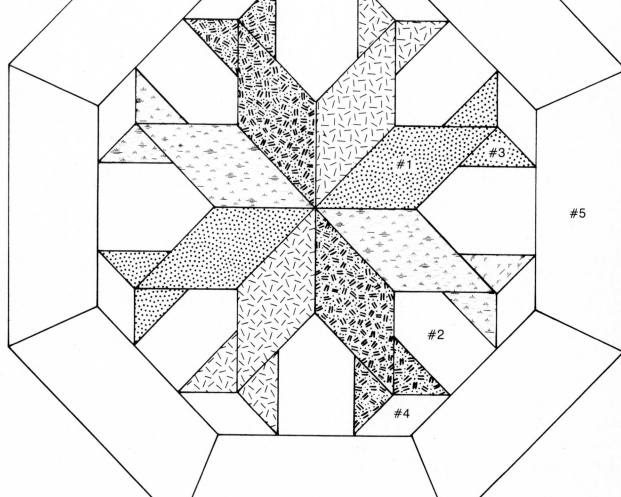

#1

#3

#5

#2

#4

Full-size pattern. Cut apart and add seams.

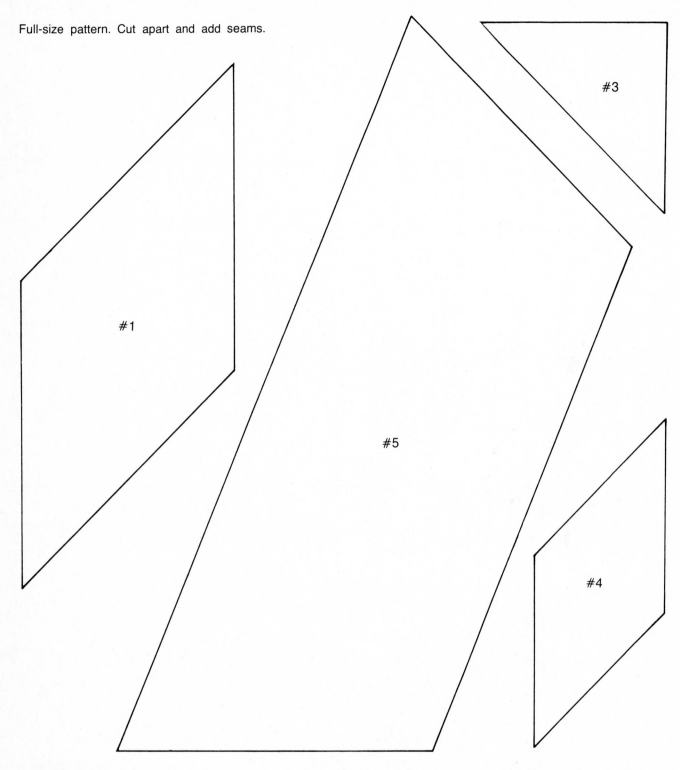

Framing Patchwork In A Hoop

Star designs and some other familiar patterns, especially those based on octagons and hexagons, fit perfectly in a round wooden embroidery hoop. Here are Sally's directions for framing:
1. Stain or paint outer ring of hoop, varnish.
2. Piece to be framed should be at least 4 inches larger than hoop for ease in pulling taut.
3. Center quilted piece in hoop and tighten outer ring.
4. Pull all layers of quilted piece very taut.
5. Very gently slide outer ring about $\frac{1}{16}$ inch toward front.
6. With single edge razor blade or art knife, cut away excess fabric.
7. Run bead of white glue all around edge of fabric, which should be showing $\frac{1}{16}$ inch at back. Slide outer hoop back in place and let dry.

NOTE: The square frame can be constructed from a do-it-yourself wooden framing kit, available at art stores. Use fabric, batting, and white glue to make the kind of covering Sally did.

Pine Tree

Each 12-inch block of this lovely delicate design contains 124 pieces! That
may explain why the quilt was originally
a group effort in Tampa. Sally shows an
easy alternative—just do one block and
frame it.

For each block cut:
   3 muslin #1
   1 muslin #2
   1 muslin #2A
   1 dark #3
   1 dark #4
   2 dark #5
   5 muslin #6
  50 muslin #7
  60 print #7

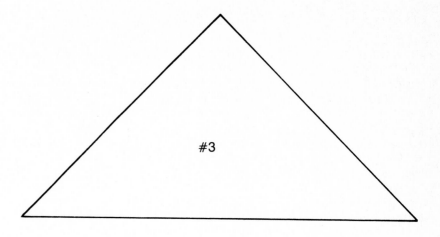

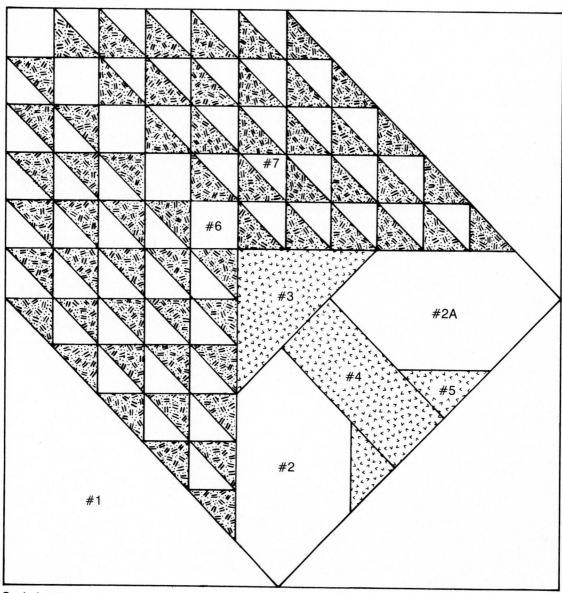

Scaled pattern.

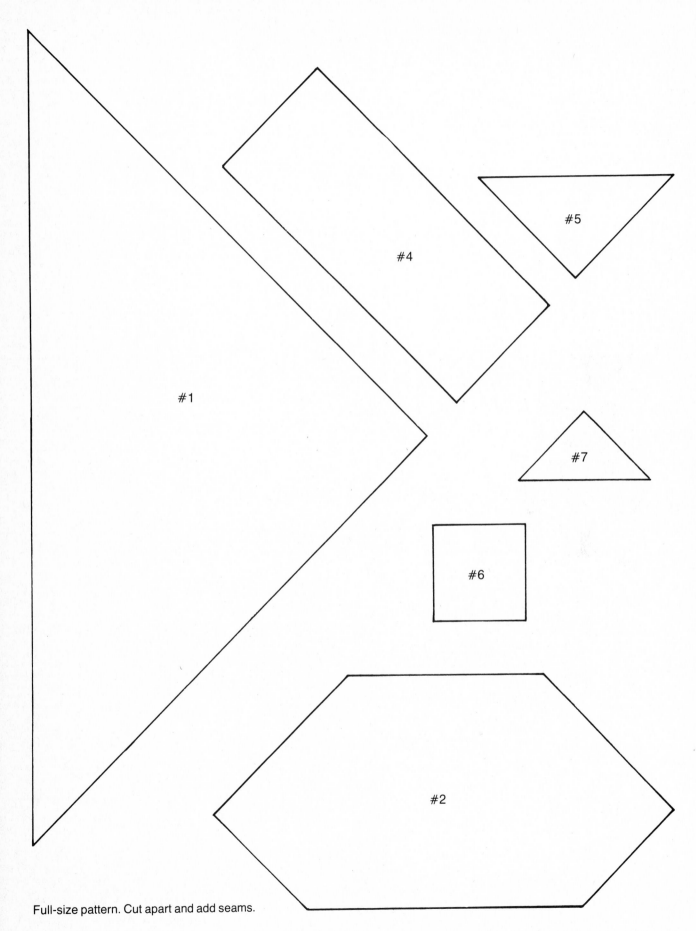

#1

#4

#5

#7

#6

#2

Full-size pattern. Cut apart and add seams.

Dove In The Window

Sally set her doves in a circle, shown by the dotted line. Feeling that you might want to use the pattern for a quilt block, we extended it into a square—the block size 11 inches square. If you plan to use it as a framed circle to fit the hoop, you will need to cut another circle of fabric plus the necessary 4 inches Sally suggests. The pieced circle can be appliquéd onto the larger circle or set into it.

For each 11-inch block cut:
    4   muslin #1
    2   print #1A
    2   print #1B
  24   muslin #2
    8   print #2A
    8   print #2B
    4   dark #3
    4   dark #3A

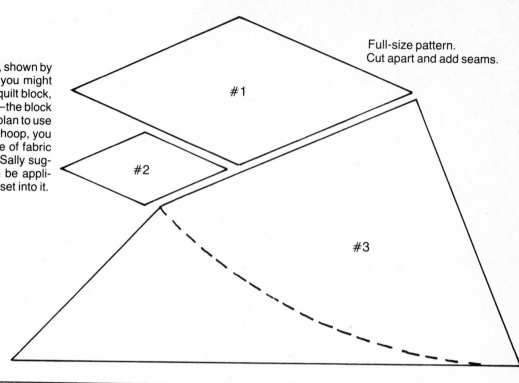

Full-size pattern.
Cut apart and add seams.

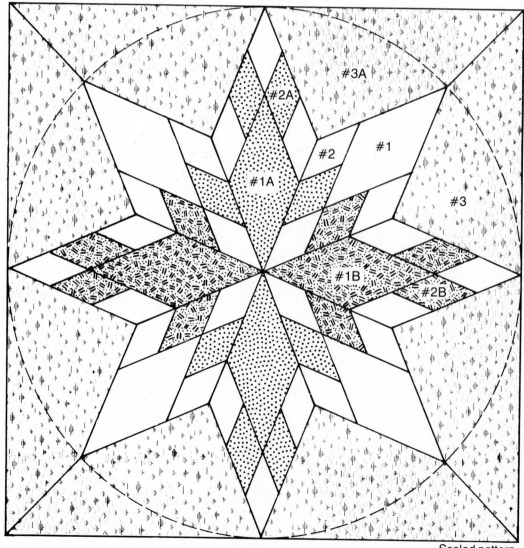

Scaled pattern.

20

Variable Star

The colors go from cool to hot in this merry mix-up. They are not as much "scrap bag" as they might seem and it takes a good eye for color to make so many pieces and secondary designs behave.

For each 15-inch star block cut:
   1 dark #1, 5-inch square, add seams
   4 light #2, 5-inch square, add seams
   4 light #3
   4 medium #3
   8 dark #3

For stripe block cut:
   12 strips #4, 2½ by 15 inches, add seams

For check block cut:
   36 squares #5, 2½ by 2½ inches, add seams

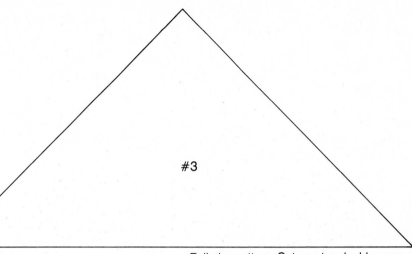

#3

Full-size pattern. Cut apart and add seams.

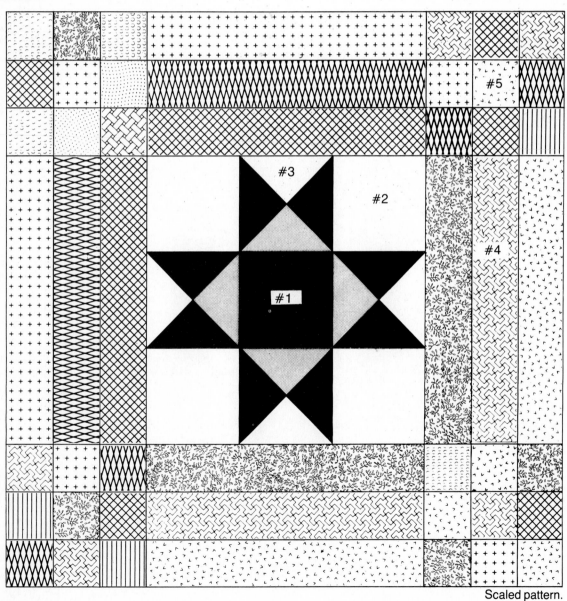

Scaled pattern.

21

Sunflower

A whirling, swirling Sunflower requires some expert piecing. In the original, the small green center circle is appliquéd with a buttonhole stitch onto the white circle. The entire circular piece may be set into the white background or the #8 pieces may be omitted and the flower appliquéd onto the 17-inch white block.

The super sashes are made up of blocks of thirty-six #9 pieces set together with the 6-inch triangles. Mathematically they should work out to fit, as shown, along the 17-inch (finished size) blocks so that the sash pieces form their own corner blocks with the checkerboard design.

The 5-inch white border is delicately appliquéd with #10 tulips and #11 leaves on a winding ⅜-inch (finished) bias vine. The edge is neatly bound.

For each block cut:
  1 green #1
  1 white #2
  8 red #3
  8 white #4
  8 gold #5
  8 white #6
  8 green #7
  8 white #8 (optional)

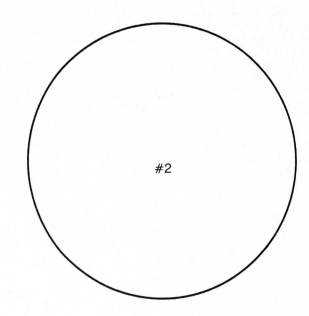

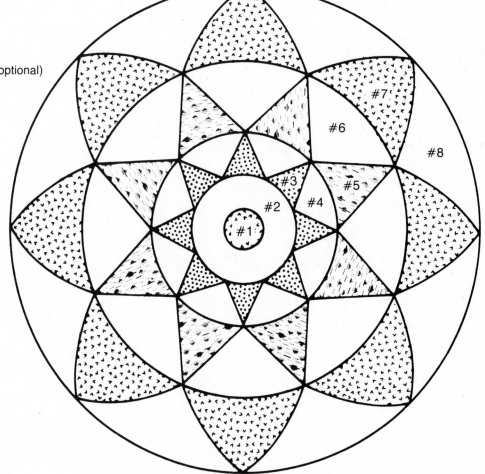

Scaled pattern.

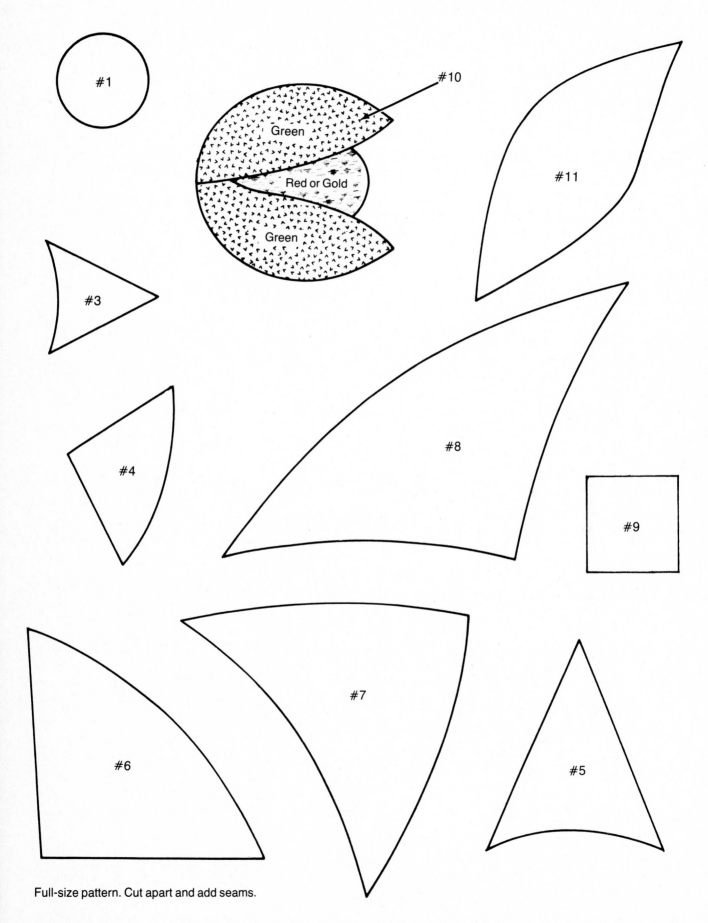

#1

#10

Green

Red or Gold

Green

#11

#3

#4

#8

#9

#6

#7

#5

Full-size pattern. Cut apart and add seams.

New York Beauty

There are three distinct patterns, block, corner block, and sash, making up this elaborate beauty. This one is for experts only. New York Beauty could also be done in very muted colors and some parts could be scrap-bag pieces. Everything, including the sashes, must be pieced, then joined.

The quilting design in the corners could be used in the Reel center of the block in a more elaborate form.

For each main block cut:
    1 medium #1
  52 print #2
  56 light #3
    4 light #4

For each corner block cut:
    1 print #5
    1 medium #6
  11 light #7
  11 print #8

For sashes cut:
  Print #9 and #10
  Light #11

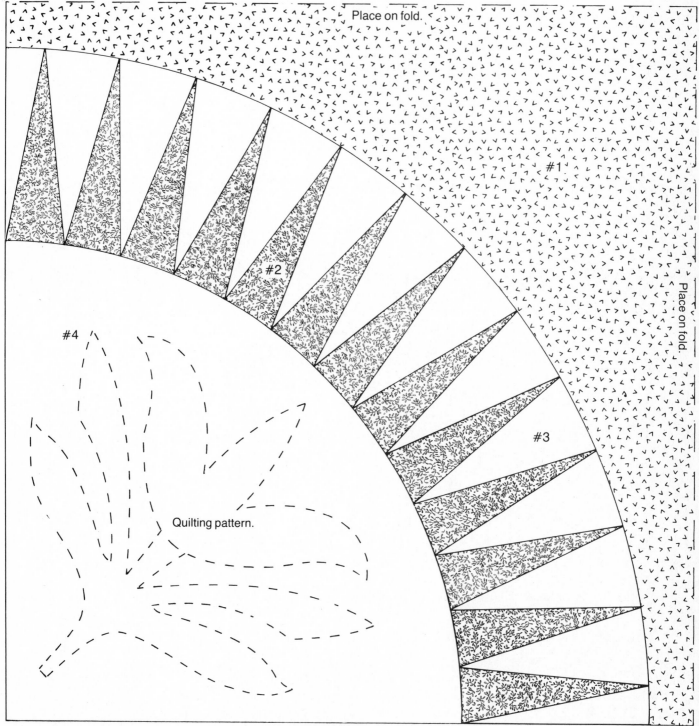

Place on fold.

Place on fold.

Full-size one-quarter main block pattern. Cut apart and add seams.

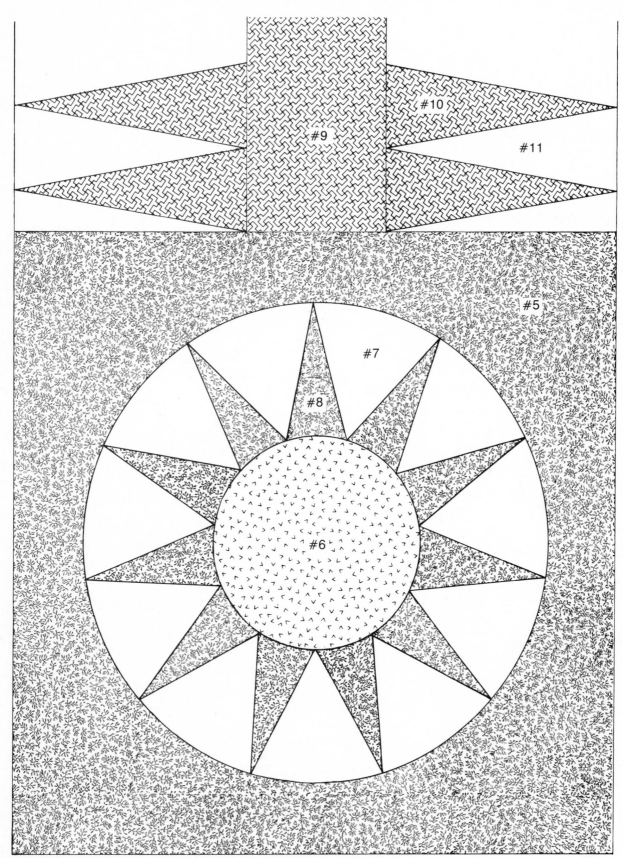

Full-size corner block and beginning of sash pattern. Cut apart and add seams.

October Foliage

(arrangement courtesy of Mary Schafer)

The abstract whirling leaves of October Foliage must be laid carefully on the fold lines of the diagram and basted securely so that the circle is smooth and unbroken. Mary placed them on white 14-inch blocks, hung diagonally and alternating with solid white blocks that leave plenty of room for her exquisite quilting. The two triangular quilting patterns can be multiplied into squares and used, or any standard wreath is suitable. The border is 12 inches wide and the special border quilting pattern goes inside the appliquéd vine.

For each block cut:
   6 print leaf designs #1
   1 print center circle #2

For border cut:
   ⅝-inch bias band
   leaf #3 and grapes #4

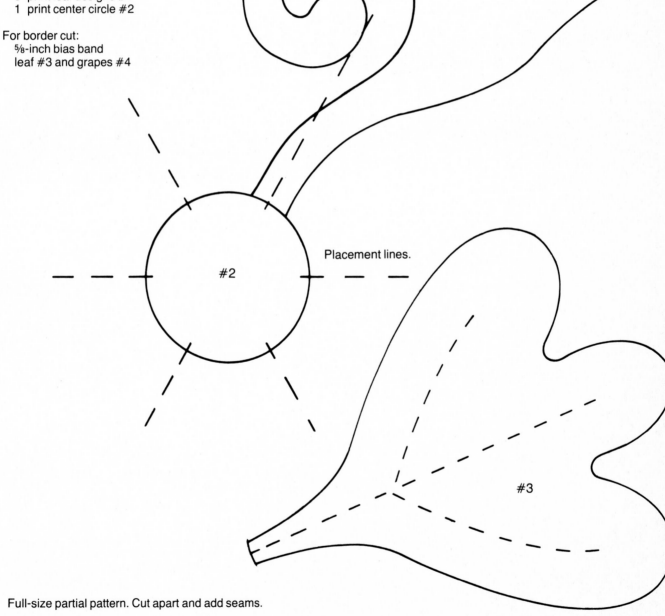

#1

#2

Placement lines.

#3

Full-size partial pattern. Cut apart and add seams.

26

Scaled pattern.

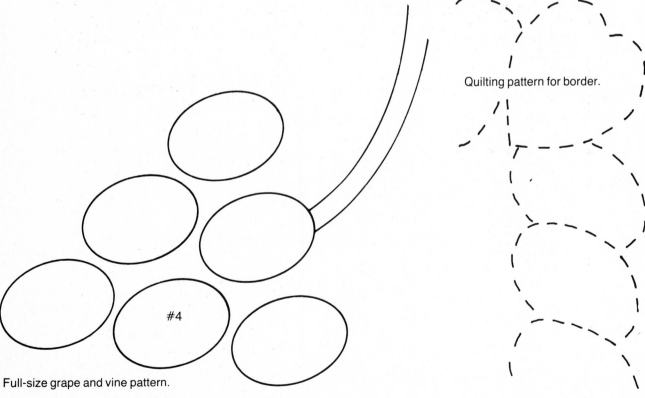

Quilting pattern for border.

#4

Full-size grape and vine pattern.

Continued on next page

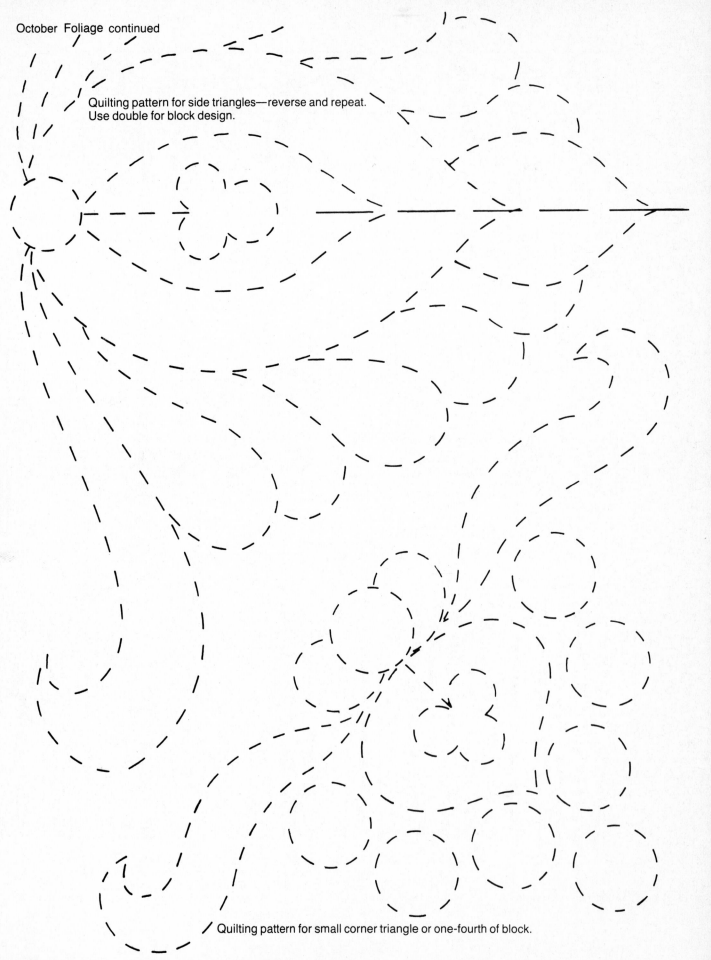

October Foliage continued

Quilting pattern for side triangles—reverse and repeat.
Use double for block design.

Quilting pattern for small corner triangle or one-fourth of block.

Delectable Mountain

Just a few miles down the road from Farmington, Maine, is The Jay Historical Society, housed in a large white federal house that was saved at the last minute from the wrecker's ball. The house is beautiful, and the furnishings, including quilts, are well worth a stop there. This Delectable Mountain (dark and light reversed from the usual) is shown in the master bedroom. Expert.
Pattern on page 30

Delectable Mountain

Accurate planning, cutting, and seaming are necessary to make Delectable Mountain as handsome as it looks in the picture. The dimensions given for the large triangles are the finished measurements along the right-angle sides—remember to add seams. You can reverse the light and dark for a more conventional arrangement. The finished quilt is 90 inches square plus an outer border (scalloped) of 5 inches or desired width.

For total quilt cut:

    1 dark #1 12¾-inch square
    8 light #2 9-inch right-angle tri-
        angles
    4 dark #2 9-inch right-angle tri-
        angles
   20 light #3 12-inch right-angle tri-
        angles
   12 dark #3 12-inch right-angle tri-
        angles

    4 dark #4 17-inch right-angle tri-
        angles
    4 dark #5 21-inch right-angle tri-
        angles
    8 light #6 15-inch right-angle tri-
        angles
   16 light #7
   16 dark #7
  160 light #8
  144 dark #8
    8 dark #9
   Enough #7, #8, and #9 for inner
        border

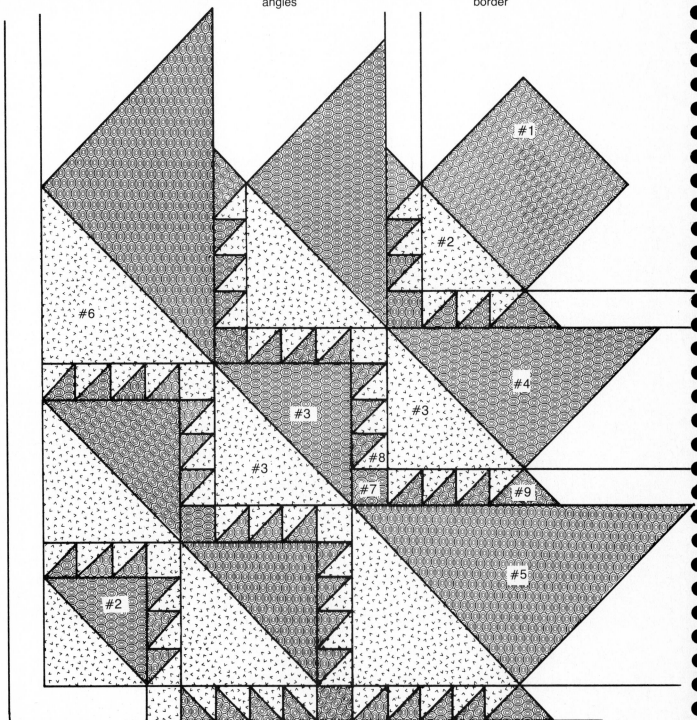

Scaled partial pattern.

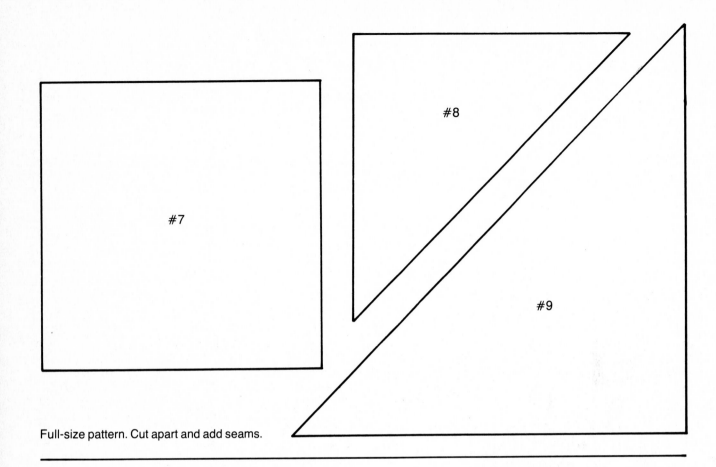

#8

#7

#9

Full-size pattern. Cut apart and add seams.

Clamshell

The bold size of Sally's Clamshell makes it easier to work with than the small Victorian size so familiar to us. Here is a pattern that can be either pieced or appliquéd. You have to be very good at piecing curves, and know just where and how to clip (as for Drunkard's Path) to piece it. Another way is to turn under the upper edge and lay it over the lower edge, appliquéing it in place. If the fabric is shifty and hard to handle, use a piece of paper inside when you paste the upper curve, as for English Piecing. Cut half dark and half light pieces, 18 across by 50 rows makes a full-size quilt.

Grain

Full-size pattern. Cut apart and add seams.

Budding Star

The intricate 12-inch blocks of this fine star pattern join hands at the corners, forming another central design. The muted colors sparkle with the tiny print in each one, adding light and texture to what might be somber if the fabrics were flat, solid colors. The medium and dark borders are approximately 6 inches wide each, and quilted in a bold cable pattern.

For each block cut:
     4 dark #1
     4 medium #1
     8 print #2
     8 medium #2
     4 print #3
     8 light #3
   16 light #4
     4 light #5

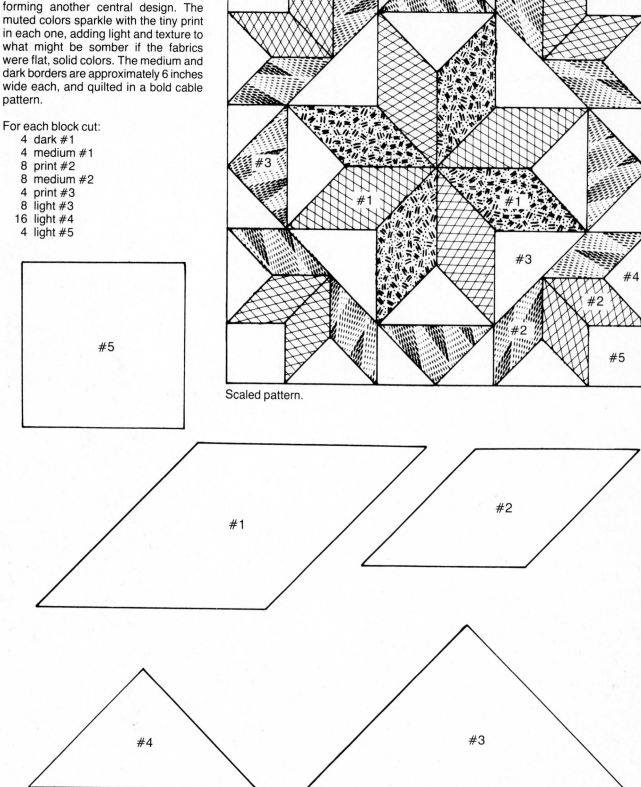

Scaled pattern.

Full-size pattern. Cut apart and add seams.

Cochise County

Cora Viola Slaughter, wife of Sheriff John Slaughter of Cochise County, was quilting out in the territory after the time the Civil War raged in the East. Her original design shows a strong Indian influence but is finely quilted with traditional Clamshell. Her descendant, John Slaughter Green, presented the quilt to the Arizona Historical Society. Expert.
Pattern on page 4

Wiscasset Quilts

The Lincoln County Cultural and Historical Association in Wiscasset, Maine, owns these beautiful 1930 quilts. They originated in Boothbay in that state and were probably made by Miss Marion McKissick. Expert.
Blue Quilt pattern on page 6
Green Quilt pattern on page 8

Little Giant

Little Giant is shown in Sabino Canyon (a National Park in the Catalina Mountains on the edge of Tucson, Arizona) where the streams run high for a short time after each rainstorm. The rugged beauty of the landscape seems to have been created for and by giants, suitable to this intricate design worked by Pat Smith. Expert. Pattern on page 10

Feathered Star

Barbara Betts of Montour Falls, New York, owns this Feathered Star variation, which she calls the Christmas Star. It was given to her by the family of the maker, Carolina Slocum, who signed and dated her work in 1851. It is shown in the house, built at the base of the falls in 1835. Expert.
Pattern on page 14

Star Of Bethlehem

The DeWitt Historical Society in Ithaca, New York is fortunate to have an unusual Star Of Bethlehem, made in 1850 by Mrs. Jared Tremen Newman. The originality and joy shown in the design blend perfectly with the many delightful fabrics. No pattern.

Fish, Pine, And Doves

Sally Tanner makes lovely hoop-framed pictures of quilt squares—seen here floating on their monofilament lines by the Shorecrest Canal in Tampa, Florida. Expert.

Fish Circle Pattern on page 16
Framing Instructions on page 17
Pine Tree Pattern on page 18
Dove In The Window Pattern on page 20

Variable Star

Phyllis Varineau studied Clothing and Textiles at The University of Utah. By pure accident she started quilting (not expecting to like it). Her first quilts were classic designs but soon the color took off in wonderful directions. This Variable Star is set with multiple sashes and corner blocks, creating a secondary design, and increasing the effect of riotous color. Expert.
Pattern on page 21

Sunflower

The three Gaddy sisters of Anson County, North Carolina, pieced and appliquéd this turn-of-the-century quilt, now owned by their great-great-niece, Rose Compton. The change in shade of the solid green fabric in the sashes and borders may be a clue that it was started at one time and finished at a later date. The setting is Burwell Hall at Queens College, North Carolina. Expert.
Pattern on page 22

40

New York Beauty

This version of Indian Summer, reflects the strong, bright colors of Arizona more than any image of New York. It was finished on August 1, 1855 by Edna Herston and presented to the Arizona Museum in Phoenix by her great-grandson, Michael DeVinney. Expert.
Pattern on page 24

October Foliage

Mary Schafer is seated in The Whaley House with her October Foliage quilt. As the leaves come whirling down, grapes ripen on the vine, and Mary catches the spirit of the harvest season in her border. Expert.
Pattern on page 26

Clamshell

Sally Wolff is shown with her Clamshell Friendship quilt on the frame her father made for her mother. The quilt has fifty-eight different red prints, many donated by friends, with several embroidered signatures. Intermediate.
Clamshell pattern on page 31

Scandinavian Folk Art

Fran Soika is a well-known quilter and teacher, as well as designer, from Novelty, Ohio. She based her Scandinavian Peasant Quilt on designs that were meant for use on painted furniture. No pattern.

Budding Star

Seen in the Loren Andrus House is Aileen Stannis' Budding Star, winner of the Best in Show —and this is only her second full-size quilt. Intermediate.
Pattern on page 32

Hands All Around ▽

The Mayflower House (Edward Winslow's House) in Plymouth, Massachusetts, has magnificent furnishings to go with its nice collection of quilts. The 19th-century fabrics in the Hands All Around are in good condition and the colors seem quite true and unfaded. Intermediate.
Pattern on page 65

◁ Autograph Cross

A country quilt with autograph blocks, made in 1872, is among the treasures at the Claflin-Richards House in Wenham. The fabrics are a delight, all the bits and pieces of a family or a community, a hundred years ago or more. Beginner.
Pattern on page 66

Crewel Blocks ▷

Also in the Claflin-Richards House is this crewel quilt, probably very early 19th century. The alternate squares are a red and blue block print, and the blue border triangles are linen. No pattern.

Pieced Rose

Pat Ashburn of Dade City not only makes quilts and teaches quilting, but, like many of us, became hooked on collecting and bought this fine 1930's pastel Pieced Rose. It seems to us almost the perfect Florida quilt with its pale, soothing colors and floral design. Intermediate.
Pattern on page 67

◁ Star And Block

Ideal for an album quilt, the Star And Block design from the Stinchfield collection is probably pre-1850, judging from the fabrics. Beginner.
Pattern on page 68

Peony ▷

In Mr. Stinchfield's collection is this Peony quilt (he says it's pronounced "pie-ony" in those parts) from the Greenwood family. It was made for Chester Greenwood, a well-known inventor, by his grandmother, some 150 years ago.
Intermediate.
Pattern on page 70

The Papago quilt was made by Mrs. Goldie Richmond to celebrate the life of her people. It won First Prize in the Arizona State Fair in 1966 and is now in the collection of the Arizona State Museum at the University in Tucson. No pattern.

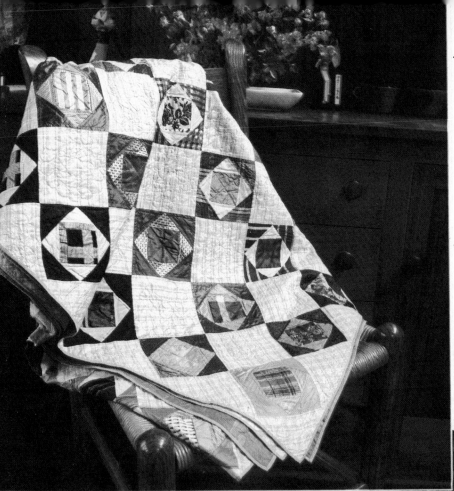

◁ Diamonds And Squares

Mary McCurdy was fortunate in that she inherited family quilts made by Mary Lewis of Delaware (1796-1864). The pieced-silk quilts and throws of the mid-19th century are fragile creations, but this Diamonds And Squares has fared well and its colors still glow. Beginner.
Pattern on page 78

▽ Rose Of Sharon

Another Mary Lewis quilt, originating in Delaware, and true to the designs and work of that area—more delicate and indicative of an easier life than the North Carolina ones of the same period—this Rose Of Sharon is transplanted to the home of its owner, Mary McCurdy. The quilting in all of the Mary Lewis quilts is fine and close and the batt much thinner than in country quilts. Intermediate.
Pattern on page 74

Sawtooth Hexagon

Annamae Kelly rescued this Sawtooth Hexagon top from a garage sale and quilted it for posterity. It is a true country quilt, completely at home in the soft morning light against old unpainted wooden barns. Intermediate.
Pattern on page 76

Tree Of Life

A Tree Of Life in decorator fabrics simulates the Palampore quilts of the 18th century in a way suited to today's living. The background is "dressmaker homespun," a rough-textured, off-white cotton. The parts of the tree and the border swags are combined prints, cut out, rearranged, and appliquéd with a fine buttonhole stitch. The hill on which the tree stands is made of Clamshell pieces. The solid border exactly fits the surface of a three-quarter bed. Sally Wolff.
Clamshell patten on page 31

Appliqué Original

Phyllis Varineau calls her coat "Disguise With Salamanders," setting her original applique on the Folkwear Turkish Coat pattern. Its colors blend with those of the restored adobe house in The Presidio in Tucson. The blue door, a cooling contrast to the warmer colors, is traditional on such houses. No pattern. Phyllis Varineau 1979 ©

Silk And Velvet

When Easterners moved west, Victoriana moved with them, picking up some interesting local touches in each area. A handsome silk and velvet throw from the Flood family proclaims its origin as Nogales, A.T. (Arizona Territory). The ubiquitous Kate Greenaway girl is joined by an Indian with a bow and arrow. The quilt is dated at the ends, 1875 and 1887. No pattern.

Victorian
Classic

The Schuyler County Historical Society in Montour Falls, New York, boasts a classic example of the Victorian throw. The border is worked so precisely that at first it might be mistaken for machine embroidery, especially the tiny buttonholed scallops. Note the elaborate spider web. No pattern.

Victorian Patchwork

Today's use of Victorian silk and velvet—in a tiny European bolero. The flattering front is laced together with fine cord. Intermediate.
Instructions for piecing on page 79. Pattern on page 81

Love Birds

The appeal of this appliquéd Love Bird design is in the colorful combinations of flowers and leaves, birds and hearts. Intermediate.
Pattern on page 86

Scrap-Bag Variable Star

This is a scrap-bag version of the Variable Star from Bertha Vukomonovich's collection. The design is, of course, perfect for scrap-bag use—a delightful and unusual star pattern, with an interesting distribution of the colored and white triangle pieces that make up the star points. Intermediate.
Pattern on page 90

Postage Stamp Basket

The National Quilting Association's Patchwork Patter magazine put out a Totebag pattern taken from the United States quilt postage stamp. Bessie Maney translated that pattern into a full-size quilt, her first hand-pieced one. When set edge-to-edge, the blocks form interesting secondary designs. Beginner.
Pattern on page 91

Fox And Geese

A young man named Myron Taft came back from the Civil War to his home in the Finger Lakes region of New York. At a dinner party given in his honor his Aunt Emma Taft unthinkingly said, "All the good boys were killed, only the rascals lived to return home." Realizing her unkindness, she made a quilt as a peace offering. It now belongs to Zitella Wood, the granddaughter of the young man. Beginner.
Pattern on page 92

Birds In Flight

Though Pat Smith hasn't been in Arizona long, most of her quilting life has been spent there. Arizona color has already made its mark on her. She is something of a booster now for Arizona climate and has worked the sun's rays into the quilting on this Birds In Flight pattern.
Beginner.
Pattern on page 93

Streaks Of Lightning

Ben Stinchfield, a resident of the Farmington, Maine area, has collected antiques all his life, although not necessarily intentionally. These two bold geometrics, Bricks and Triangles, both arranged in a Lightning design, were in the house when he was born. They are perfect examples of 19th-century Maine utility quilts; the beautiful colors and prints are in mint condition. Beginner.
Pattern on page 94

Stearns and Foster "Famous Women" contest winner. No pattern.

Square Within A Square

May Tow appreciates the delicate miniaturism of this Victorian silk Square Within A Square from her private collection.
Beginner.
Pattern on page 96

Hands All Around

One of the oldest, tried-and-true, dear-to-the-hearts-of-group-quilters designs that has ever been worked is this variation of an Eight-Point Star, complete with signature block in the center. The block is 11¾ inches finished and is usually set with sashes, in this case about 2½ inches wide.

For each block cut:
- 1 dark #1
- 4 light #2
- 8 light #3
- 16 dark #4
- 8 light #5

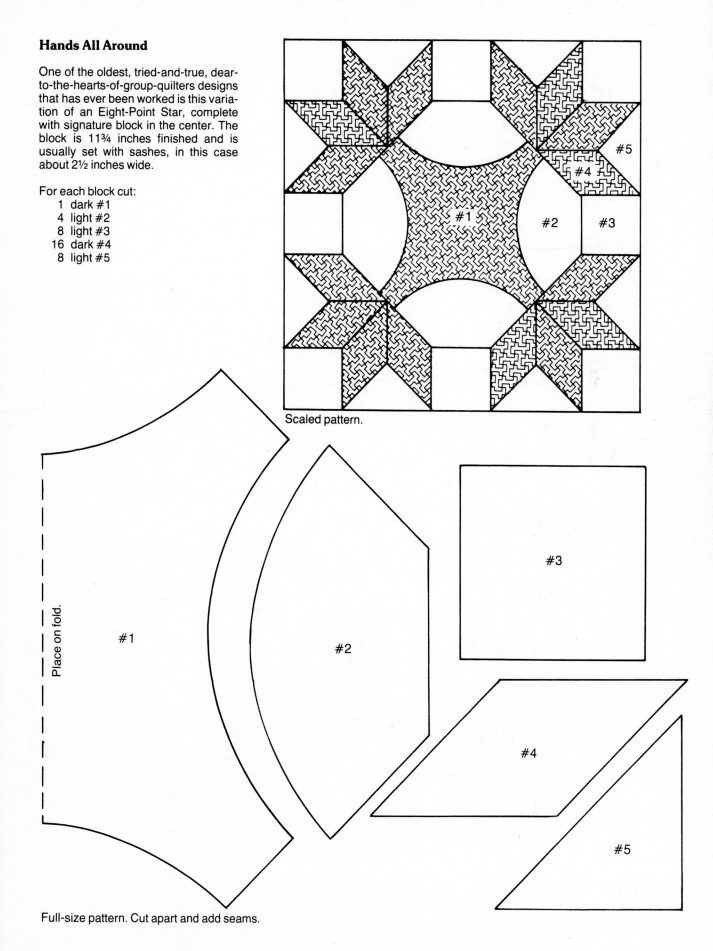

Scaled pattern.

Place on fold.

#1

#2

#3

#4

#5

Full-size pattern. Cut apart and add seams.

Autograph Cross

Not only is this a good beginner's pattern but it can be ideal for teaching a group by using scraps from each member's collection. Place an embroidered signature square in the block center. The simple 3-inch sashes are used to set the blocks diagonally. Each block is 10 inches square, 14 inches across diagonally. The edges can be finished with plain triangles, 10 inches on the right-angle sides, and a border.

For each block cut:
  1 white #1
  4 dark #2
  4 light #3

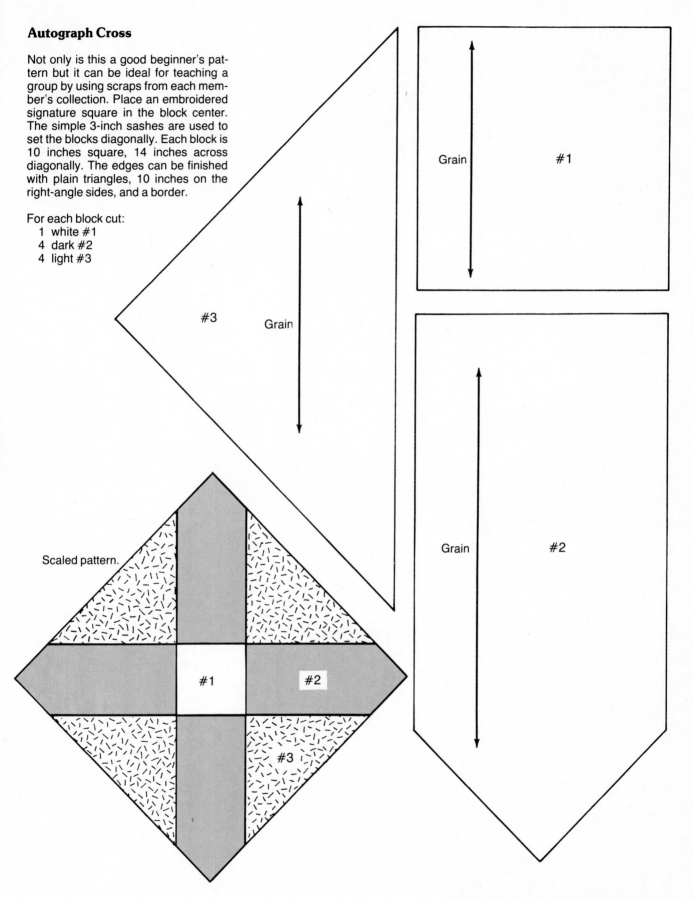

Scaled pattern.

Full-size pattern. Cut apart and add seams.

Pieced Rose

Pat Ashburn calls this 1930's design Amish Blume, in a play on words referring to her Amish origins. It is an uncomplicated and exciting pieced floral with an airy effect. The colors that are used in the original are pleasing but it could also be done in a variety of pastel print flowers with green leaves.

For each block cut:

4 pink #1	4 white #4A
4 pink #1A	4 green #5
4 white #2	4 green #5A
4 white #2A	4 white #6
4 green #3	4 white #6A
4 green #3A	1 green #7
4 white #4	

For border cut:
½ total number needed in pink #8
½ total number needed in white #8, cut at dotted line

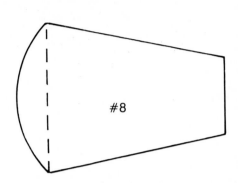

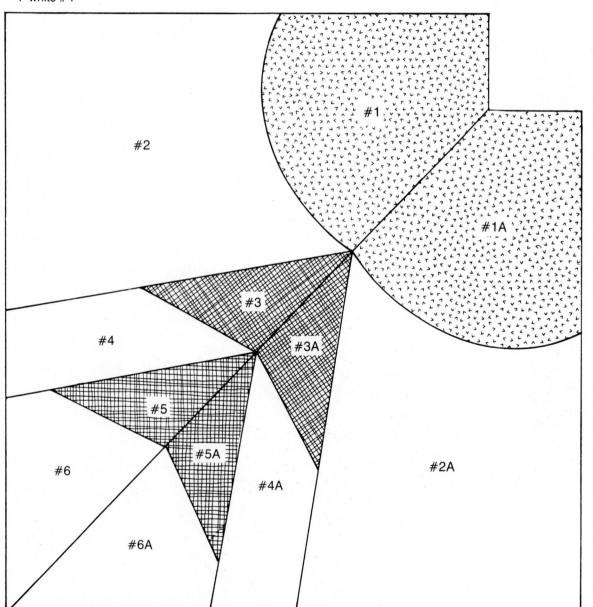

Full-size pattern for one-quarter of block. Cut apart and add seams.

Star And Block

The scaled diagram of this design is exactly half size and large enough in itself to use effectively. The double heart quilting will fit a 5-inch sashing and border, the fan quilting will fit a 4-inch width, giving you a choice in size and design.

The following measurements are for a full-size block; add seams and cut:
- 1 light #1, 4¼-inch square
- 4 light #2, 4¼ inches on right-angle sides
- 4 light #3, 3 inches on right-angle sides
- 4 light #4, 3-inch square
- 16 dark #5, 2⅛ inches on right-angle sides

For full-size sashes and borders cut:
   5-inch strips of medium color, add seams

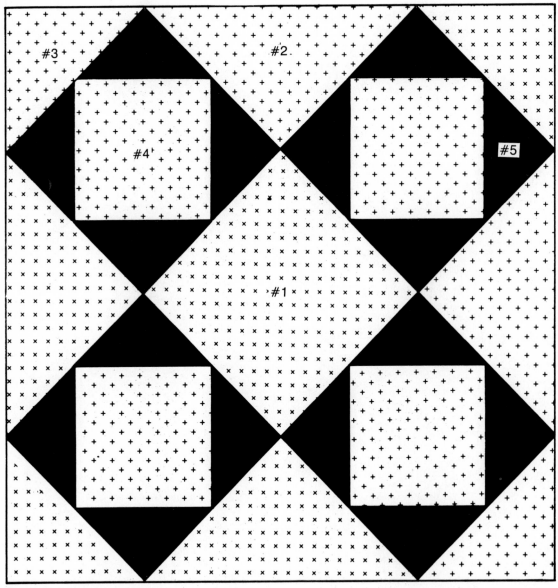

One-half size pattern.

Possible quilting patterns for sashes and borders.

Peony

The pieced and appliquéd blocks are hung diagonally in this arrangement of an old favorite. We have designed a quilted Peony for the alternating white blocks. Red petals with green leaves and stems are traditional but scrap-bag pieces might also be used for the petals. Muslin white is softer than bleached white for the background.

For each block cut:
1 white 4½-inch square, add seams
2 green #1
4 red #1
3 white #2
2 white #3
2 white #4
1 green leaf #5 and #6
6 inches of #7 green ½-inch bias, add seams

For alternate blocks cut:
9-inch white squares, add seams

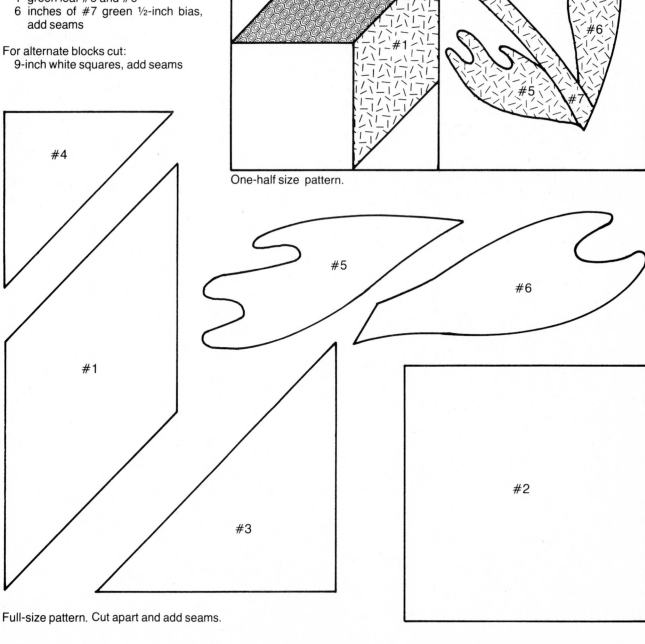

One-half size pattern.

Full-size pattern. Cut apart and add seams.

70

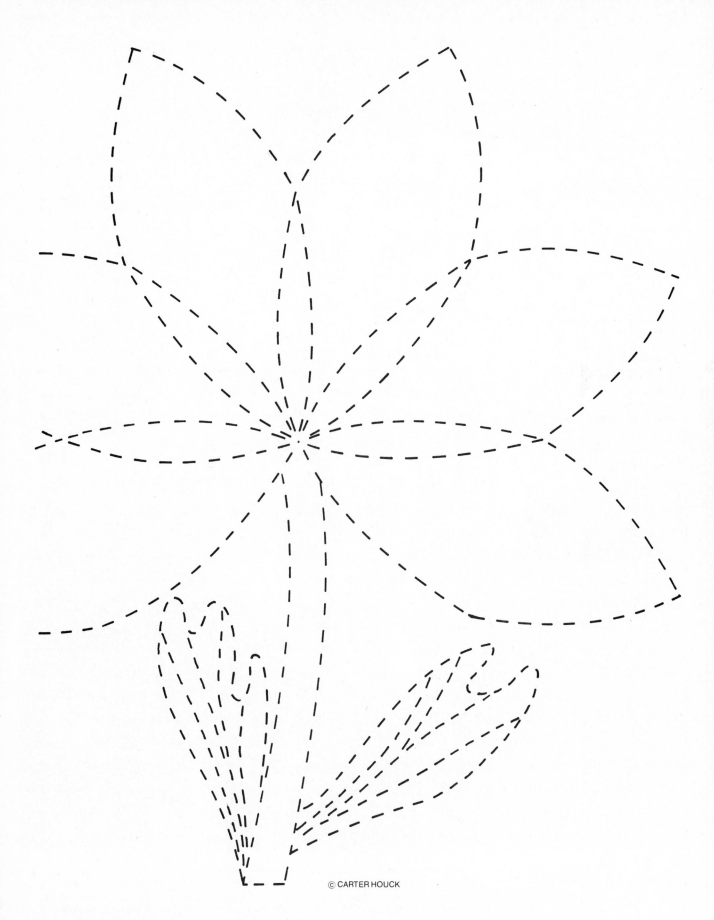

© CARTER HOUCK

Possible quilting pattern for alternate blocks.

71

Spring Beauty

This handsome Mary Lewis quilt shows her excellent quilting on a Wild Goose Chase design. The block is very similar to many others, such as Oddfellow, Rambler, and Railroad Crossing, but appears in a recent Canadian book as Spring Beauty. Many variations with imaginative names can develop from one basic design. Intermediate.

Spring Beauty

The neat polka-dot and white contrast and the diagonal setting of the blocks make this an even stronger graphic design than if it were worked in scrap-bag pieces. It has numerous possibilities for color, setting, and borders. The Saw-tooth border seen here is made from 1½-inch squares, the white sashes are 3 inches wide.

For each block cut:
- 1 white #1
- 4 dark #2
- 16 dark #3
- 24 white #4

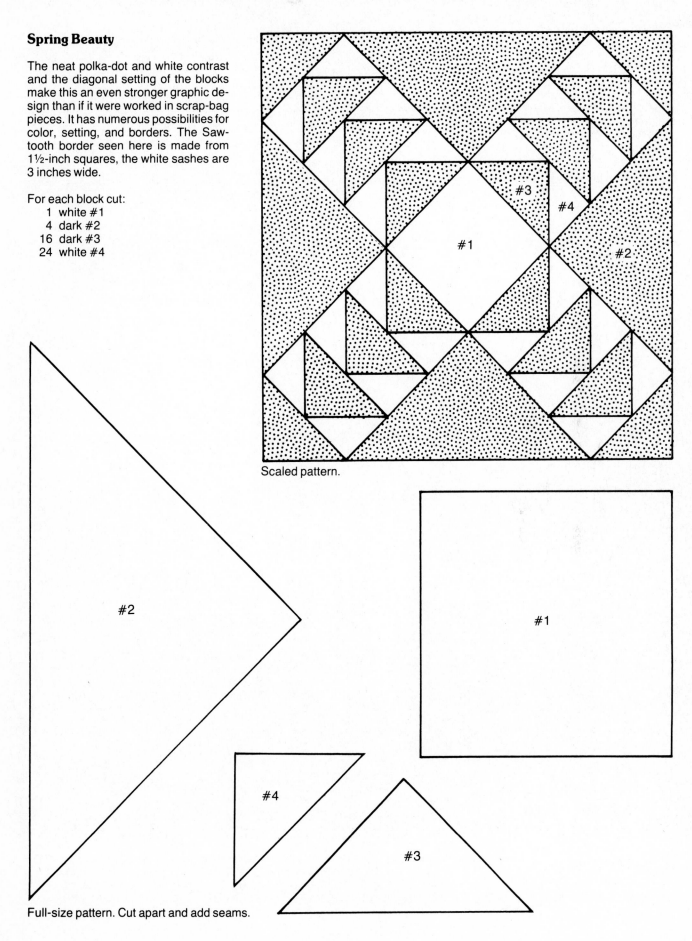

Scaled pattern.

Full-size pattern. Cut apart and add seams.

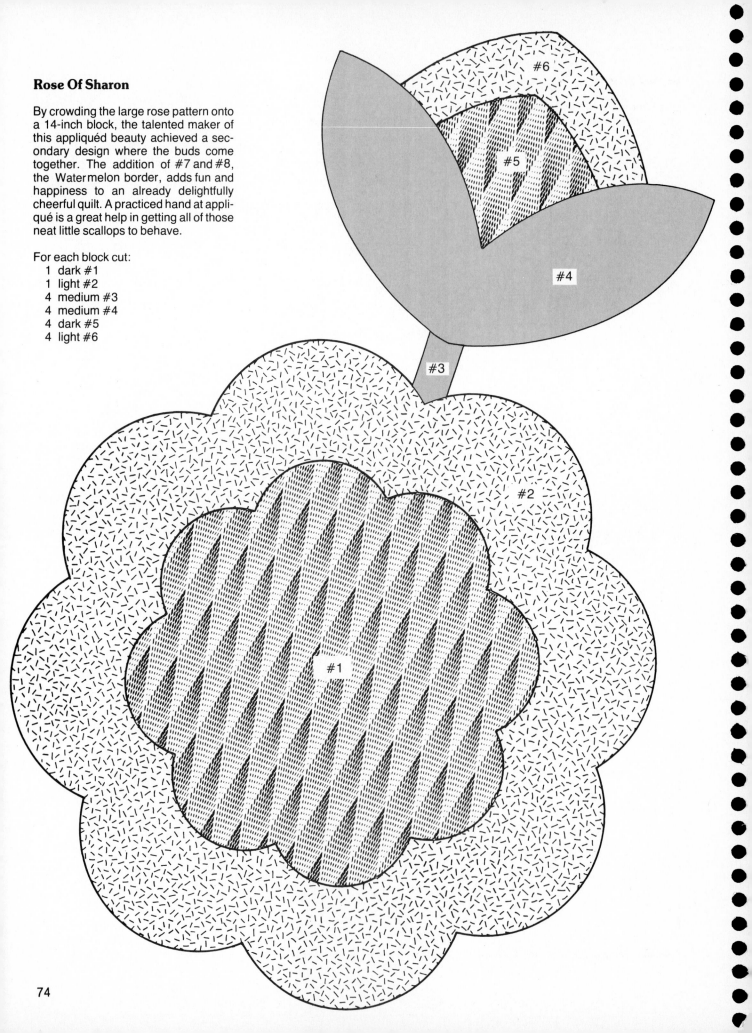

Rose Of Sharon

By crowding the large rose pattern onto a 14-inch block, the talented maker of this appliquéd beauty achieved a secondary design where the buds come together. The addition of #7 and #8, the Watermelon border, adds fun and happiness to an already delightfully cheerful quilt. A practiced hand at appliqué is a great help in getting all of those neat little scallops to behave.

For each block cut:
    1 dark #1
    1 light #2
    4 medium #3
    4 medium #4
    4 dark #5
    4 light #6

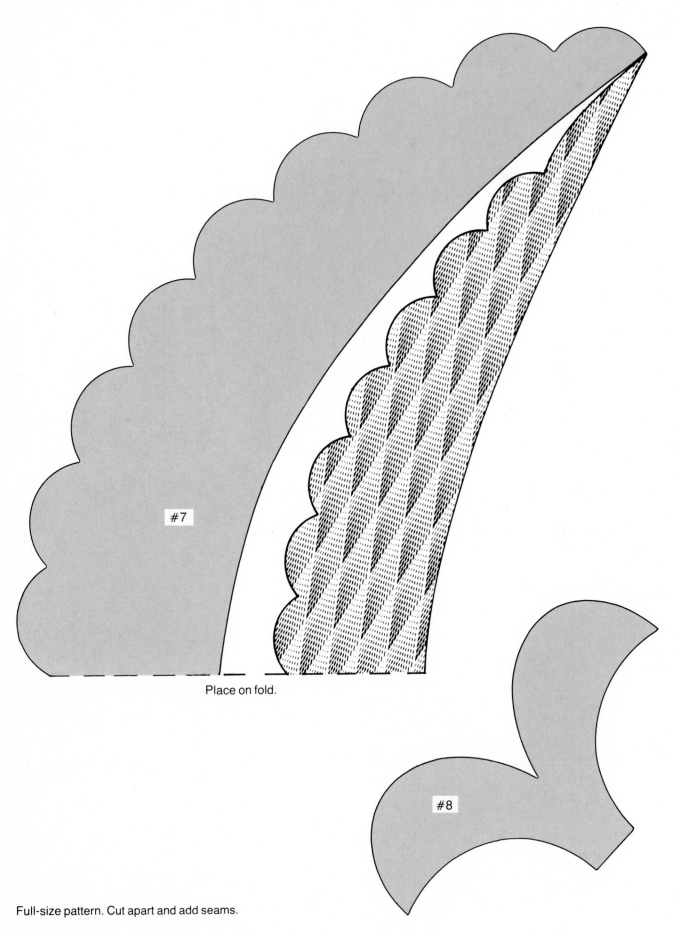

#7

Place on fold.

#8

Full-size pattern. Cut apart and add seams.

Sawtooth Hexagon

The geometry of this block design is so tricky that one wonders whether it was carefully calculated or the originator just hit upon it by doodling with squares and triangles. Any way you look at it, the effect is great. The blocks are set with the neat corner blocks made of one medium and one dark triangle, and 11-by 3½-inch sashes of a very light, small print.

For each 15-inch block cut:
   1 dark #1
  16 light #2
  16 dark #2
   8 light #3
   4 dark #4

For each corner block cut:
  1 dark #5
  1 light #5

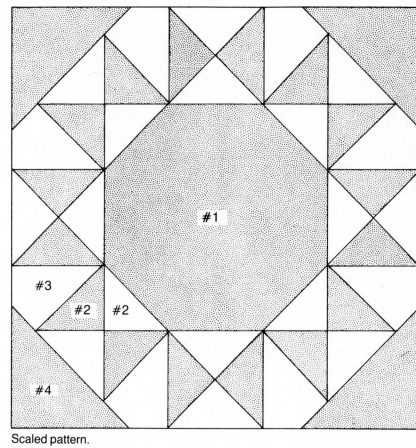

Scaled pattern.

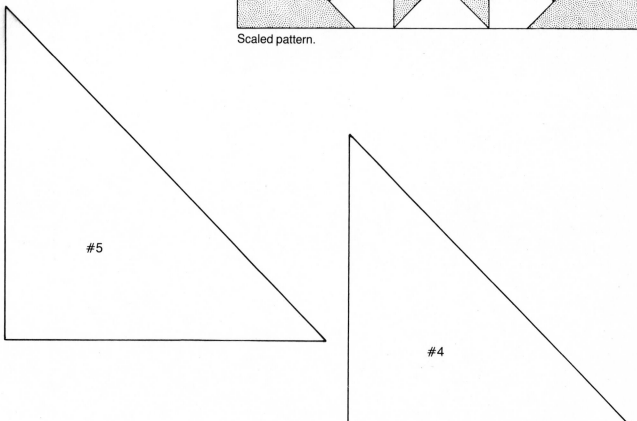

76

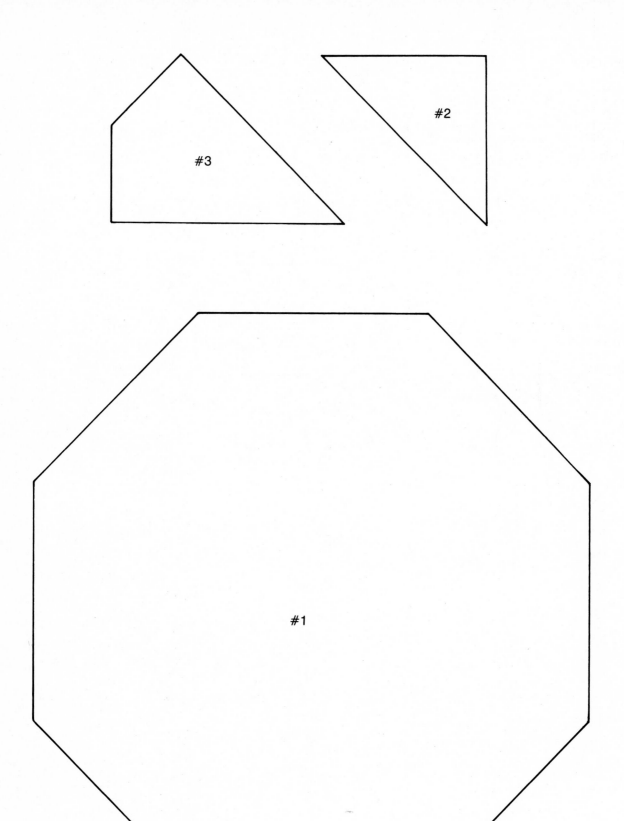

#3

#2

#1

Full-size pattern. Cut apart and add seams.

Diamonds And Squares

The delicacy of the silks in the original can be duplicated by using fine, softly colored cotton prints. The alternate quilted blocks can be made, as shown, in a pastel stripe or tiny polka dots or pale print. For a bolder and quicker quilt, you can double the size of the blocks. The diagonal arrangement is especially pleasing.

For each block cut:
- 1 dark #1
- 4 light #2
- 4 dark #3
- 1 light #4 for quilting

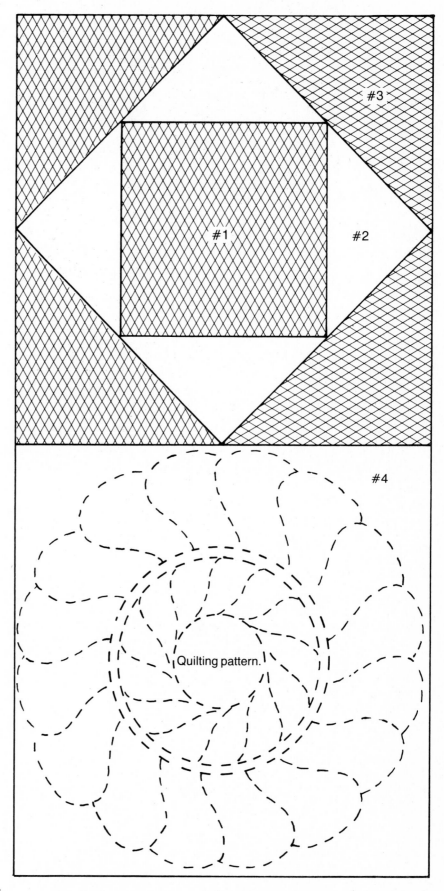

Quilting pattern.

Full-size pattern. Cut apart and add seams.

Introduction To Victorian Patchwork

Victorian patchwork begins with the collection of material. Real silk is expensive, but there are synthetics whose glow and color permit their use as substitutes. Velvet and velveteen mix well with silk. Be sure to check the nap and turn each piece of velvet or velveteen so that it will stroke upward when worn, giving the fabric the darkest and richest effect. Ribbons make very useful pieces to supplement the other fabrics.

As you collect fabrics for your project, you'll find yourself searching remnant bins, digging through flea markets, begging scraps from friends and neighbors that sew. While it is possible to use the less-worn parts of old party dresses, ascots, scarfs, and ties, be sure they're clean and still strong enough to hold against new fabrics. An interesting alternative to silk and velvet—and easier to get—is wool and corduroy.

Thread is no real problem—six-strand embroidery floss works very well. Choose a high quality, highly mercerized brand to blend with your fine fabrics. You will use from two to four strands, depending on the size and delicacy of the fabric pieces. Silk embroidery threads are being imported from Japan; we used a medium-weight twisted silk thread in our work.

Keep in mind when planning Victorian patchwork for clothing that a pattern without darts works best. We include the small European bolero pattern shown on the following pages.

Laying Down The Base

Victorian patchwork is worked on a base—preferably unbleached, washed and ironed, all-cotton muslin. Cut the muslin piece, pin or baste it together, try the garment on for fit, and make any necessary alterations before starting the elaborate surface work.

Use a tracing wheel and carbon to mark seam lines on both sides (right and wrong) of all fabric pieces. Cut one inch beyond seam lines instead of on the usual five-eighths-inch cutting line. The heavy fabrics and embroidery stitches tend to shrink the piece slightly and you may need the extra allowance. Figure #1.

You may pre-plan the design of the pieces, using a pencil and ruler, French curve, etc. Draw directly on the muslin and erase, if necessary, with an art gum eraser. You may find that some fabric pieces do not conform exactly to your

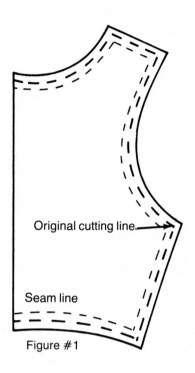

Figure #1

first design—erase and redesign. Figure #2.

You can work without a diagram. Place a few fabric pieces on the muslin, pin the pieces to the muslin, place more fabric pieces, and pin. In trimming the fabric pieces to fit, be sure to allow at least a one-half-inch overlay so that one-fourth inch can be turned under on the raw edge. Use selvages and the selvage edges of ribbons for overlap whenever possible. It is much easier and less bulky if you always place the velvets under the silks so that velvet edges don't need to be turned. Figure #3.

When you have covered a fairly large area to your satisfaction, start basting and do a lot of it. Work on a flat surface so that you can hold the muslin base firm and smooth while you baste the fabric pieces. Be sure that the pieces extend well into the seams.

Blending the colors and using the striped, printed, and embroidered pieces makes Victorian patchwork fun. The high sheen of silks and velvets makes it possible to use unusual colors together because the fabric reflects and picks up from the adjoining pieces, thus tempering the effect. Should two dull-looking pieces fall together, you can add bright embroidery thread for contrast.

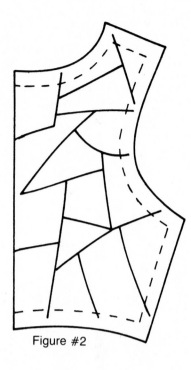

Figure #2

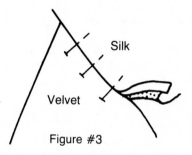

Figure #3

Embroidering

The embroidery stitches hold the pieces together and firmly to the muslin base. The embroidery stitches must encompass the edges of each piece so plan carefully; wide stitches, such as the buttonhole, herringbone, and feather stitch are obvious choices. After all fabric pieces are firmly embroidered to the muslin base, have fun with French knots, lazy daisies, and an assortment of straight stitch patterns.

Finishing Touches

With embroidered sides together, seam the bolero shoulders. Press seams open. Always test the temperature of your iron to a scrap of fabric before touching the iron to your fabric. Pressing napped fabrics such as velvet or corduroy requires extra care. Steam rather than press and you won't flatten

Continued on next page

the pile. Place a terry towel or a piece of the same fabric on the ironing board. Allow the fabric to cool and the moisture to evaporate before you move the piece about.

Cut a lining to match the altered muslin base pieces. Seam lining shoulders. Press seams open. Figure #4

Optional: On all but the underarm side seam line place a corded piping around the edges of the bolero pieces.

The seam edge of the piping should lie with the seam allowance of the vest. With a zipper or cording machine foot, stitch close to the cord. Figure #5.

If you plan to use cord loops for the ties on the bolero front, place them now. Figure #6.

With right sides together, pin, then stitch the lining and bolero together on all edges except the underarm side seam. (Use the cording foot if you used

the corded piping.) Figure #7.

Trim and clip the seams. Figure #8.

Turn the bolero right side out by pulling the front through the shoulder and out the side opening on the back. Figure #9.

If you did not use the optional piping closing, attach small purchased metal rings by hand stitching now. Finish by turning the side seams of the lining in and hand stitch. Figure #10.

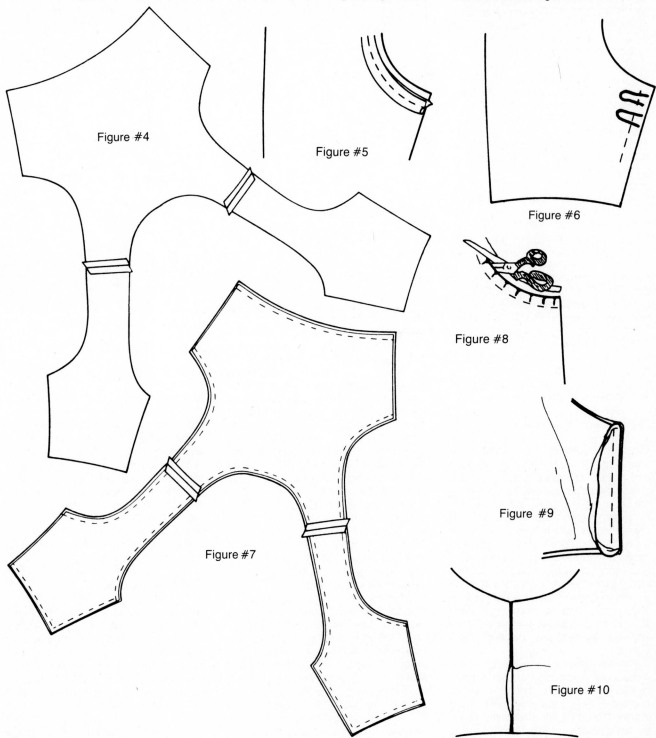

Figure #4

Figure #5

Figure #6

Figure #7

Figure #8

Figure #9

Figure #10

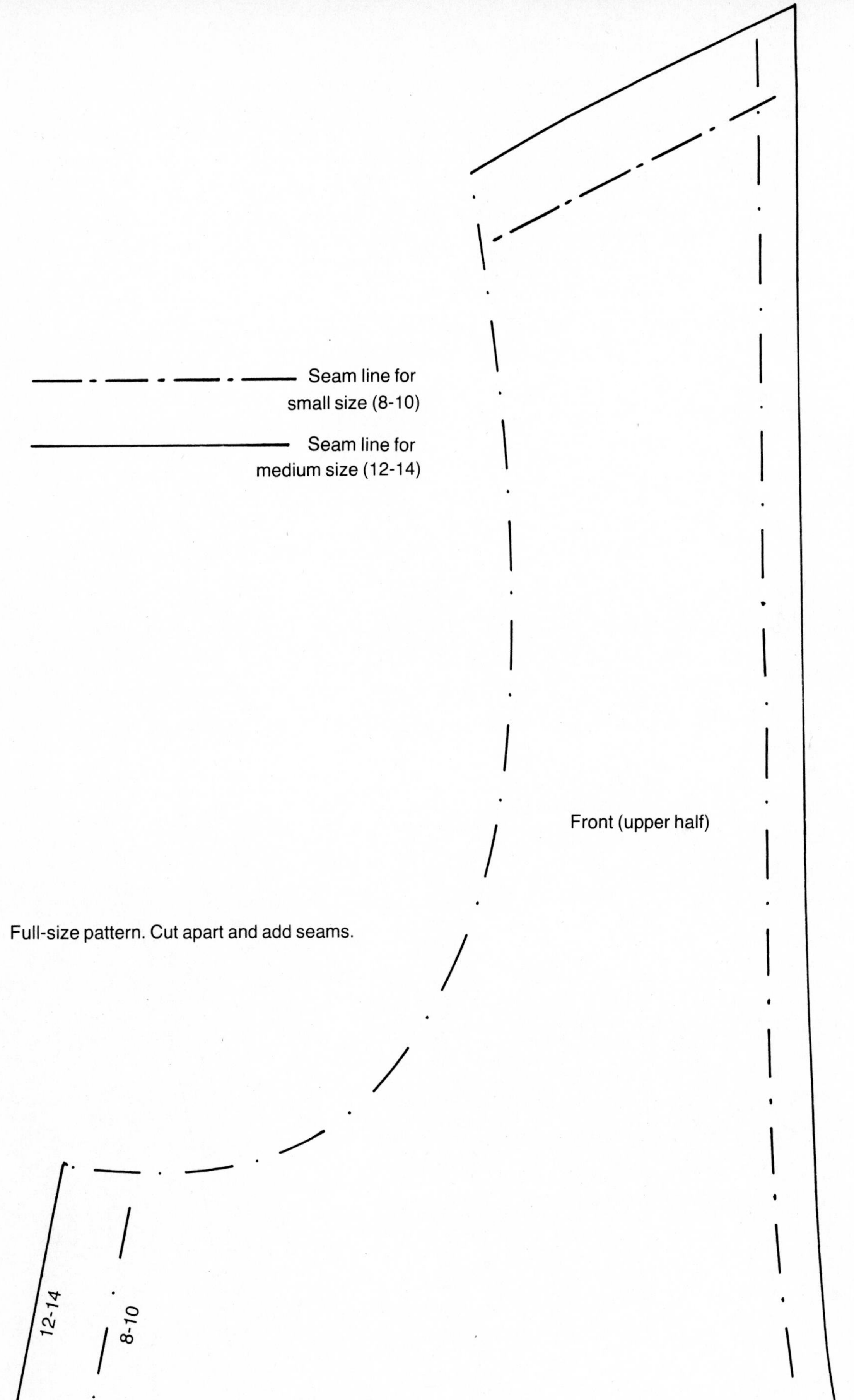

Seam line for
small size (8-10)

Seam line for
medium size (12-14)

Front (upper half)

Full-size pattern. Cut apart and add seams.

12-14

8-10

Join A

Continued on next page

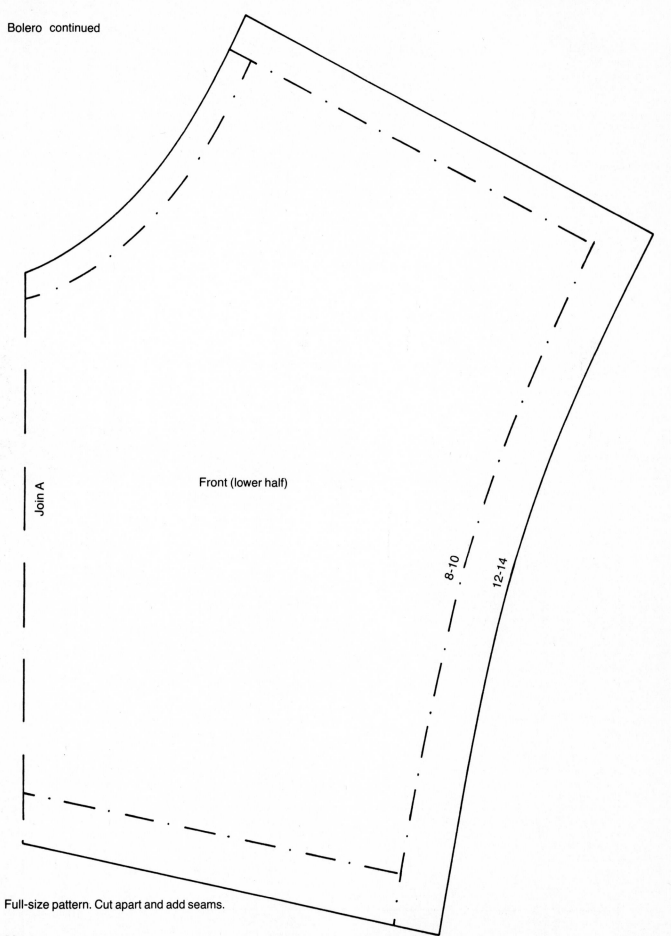

Join A

Front (lower half)

8-10

12-14

Full-size pattern. Cut apart and add seams.

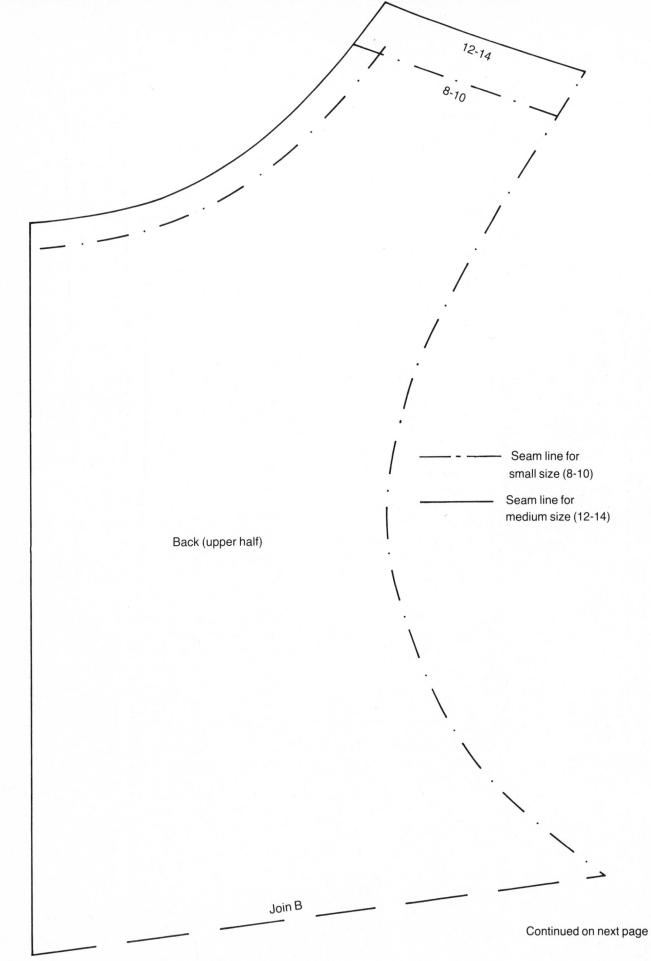

12-14

8-10

Seam line for
small size (8-10)

Seam line for
medium size (12-14)

Back (upper half)

Join B

Continued on next page

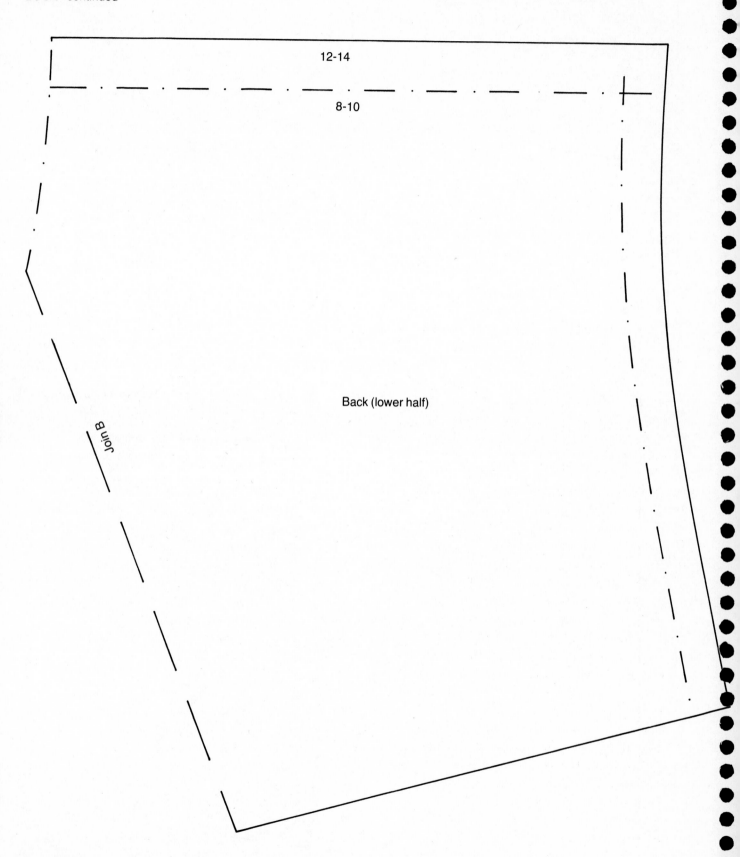

12-14

8-10

Back (lower half)

Join B

Full-size pattern. Cut apart and add seams.

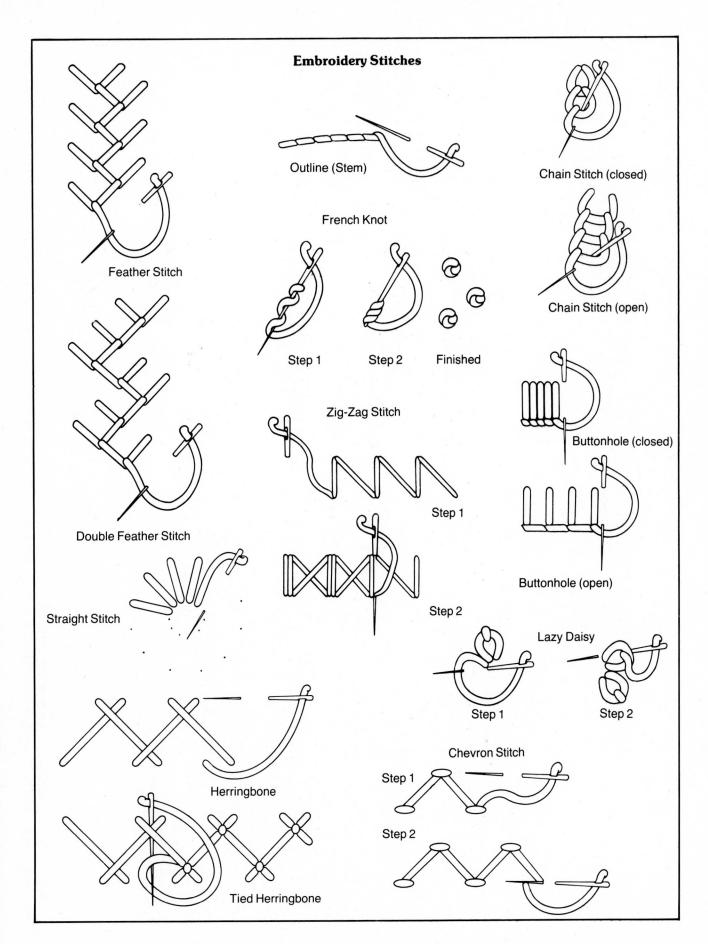

Embroidery Stitches

Outline (Stem)

Chain Stitch (closed)

French Knot

Chain Stitch (open)

Step 1   Step 2   Finished

Feather Stitch

Zig-Zag Stitch

Buttonhole (closed)

Double Feather Stitch

Step 1

Buttonhole (open)

Straight Stitch

Step 2

Lazy Daisy

Step 1   Step 2

Herringbone

Chevron Stitch

Step 1

Step 2

Tied Herringbone

Love Birds

Here's a handy appliqué pattern that you can rearrange to suit your fancy and the size of your bed. The extra birds on the pillow make it easy to create a really bed-fitting quilt.

The double bird design goes in the center of the bed. The small circle around it is made of ½-inch wide bias and leaves. The scalloped inner border is about a yard in diameter on the double bed. The larger flowers are arranged on a trailing vine (½-inch wide) bias border with the larger leaves, making a nice showy skirt around the bed.

Lay out your design carefully to fill the dimensions of your bed in a pleasing way. The very severe geometric type of quilting is an attractive contrast to the curving appliqué. You may use the appliqué designs for quilting to create echoing shadow wreaths or a back-ground of scattered flowers or large triangular bouquets in the corners.

For center birds cut:
- 2 medium #1
- 2 dark #2
- 2 light #3
- 1 medium #4
- 2 medium #5
- 1 medium #6
- 1 print #7
- 2 print #8
- 2 dark #9
- 14 dark #10

For each heart motif cut:
- 2 light #10
- 1 medium #11
- 1 print #12

For each tulip motif cut:
- 4 dark #10
- 1 medium #13

For each flower motif cut:
- 1 dark #14
- 1 light #15

For pillow birds cut:
- 1 medium #13
- 3 medium #10
- 2 medium #17
- 2 dark #18
- 2 light #19
- 2 print #20
- 10 light #21
- 10 dark #22
- 6 dark #23

For each skirt flower cut:
- 6 dark #23
- 1 print #24
- 1 medium #25
- 1 dark #26
- 1 medium #27
- 1 dark #28

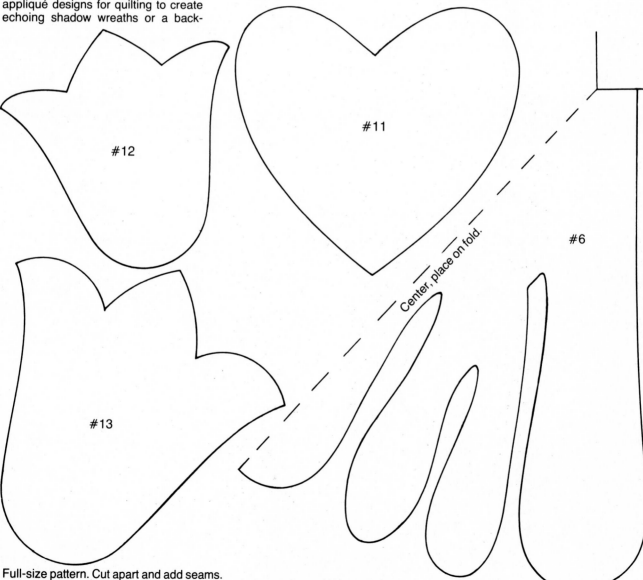

#12

#11

#13

Center, place on fold.

#6

Full-size pattern. Cut apart and add seams.

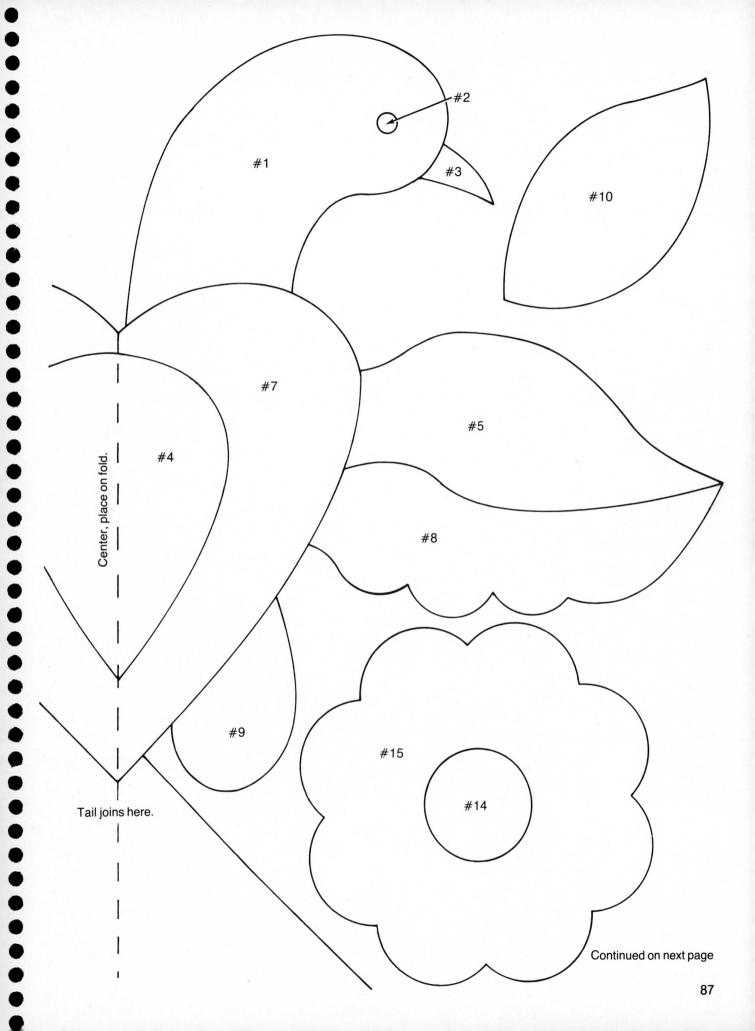

#2

#1

#3

#10

#7

#5

Center, place on fold.

#4

#8

#9

#15

#14

Tail joins here.

Continued on next page

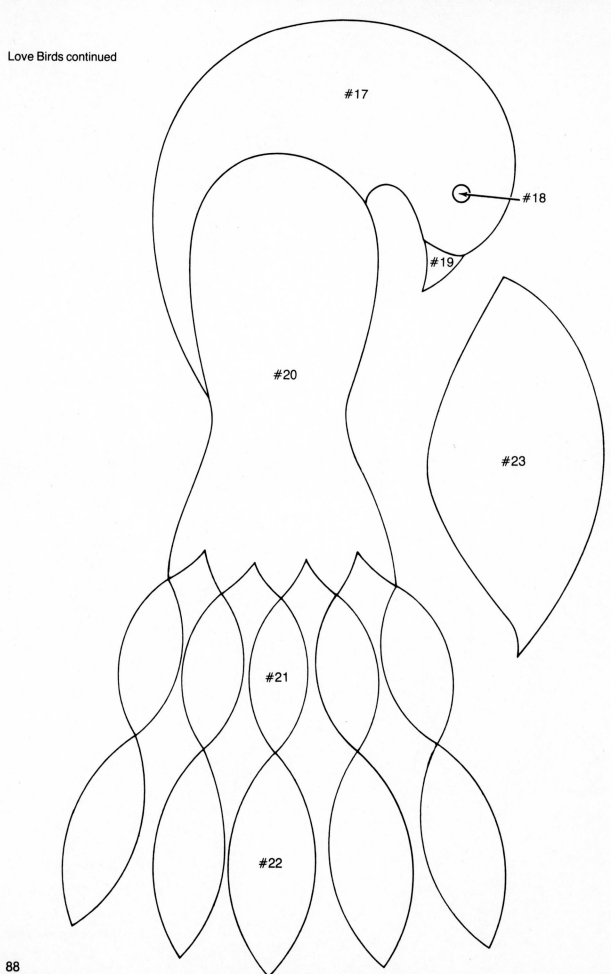

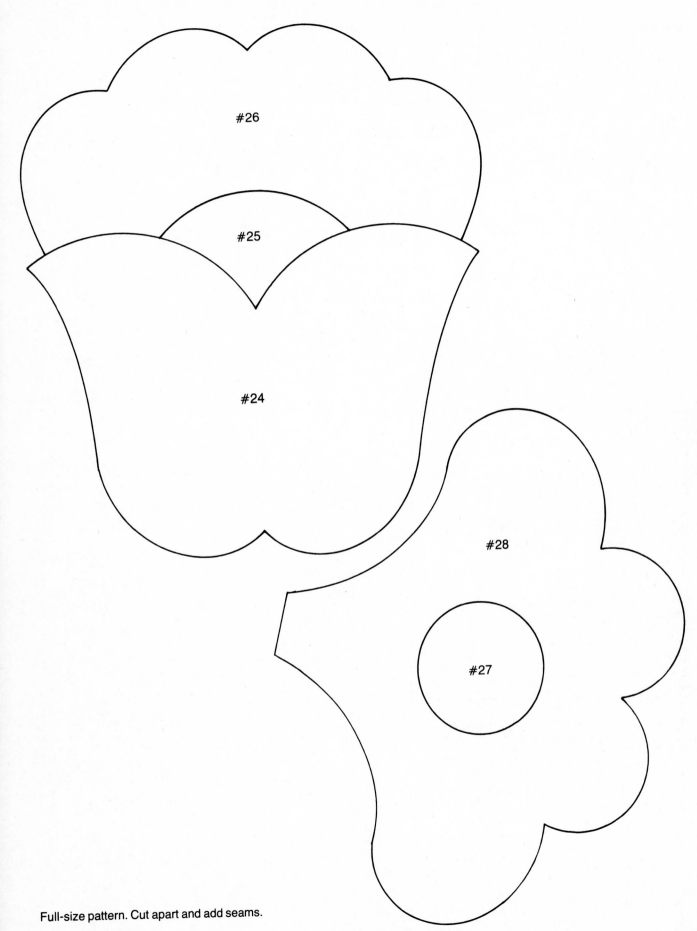

#26

#25

#24

#28

#27

Full-size pattern. Cut apart and add seams.

Scrap-Bag Variable Star

Here the Variable Star reaches its most infinite variety. Muslin and scrap-bag pieces are all that's needed. The pattern, as given, works out to a 12-inch block, but it's an easy one to increase.

For each block cut:
- 4 white #1
- 4 white #2
- 4 white #3
- 24 white #4
- 84 colored #4

For sash cut 1½-inch × 12-inch strips, add seams.

For corner blocks cut 1½-inch squares, add seams.

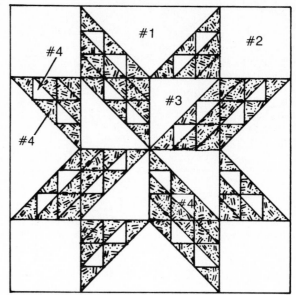

Scaled pattern.

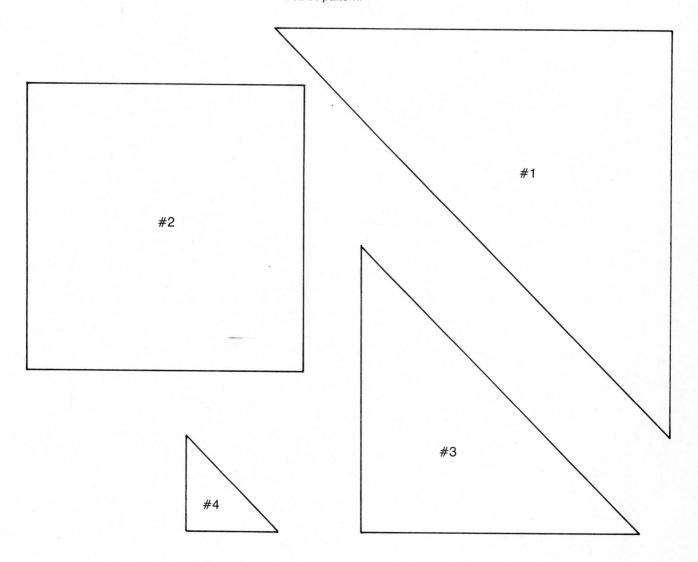

Full-size pattern. Cut apart and add seams.

90

Postage Stamp Basket

Arranged exactly like it was on the sheet of United States stamps, but done in brighter colors, this little basket creates several patterns and designs so that it becomes hard to tell which is the center of a block. Each block is made up of four of the squares given, with the appliquéd handles turned toward each other in the center.

For each square cut:
- 2 white #1
- 1 print #1
- 2 white #2
- 2 print #3
- 1 print #4, cut to shape or shaped with a bias strip

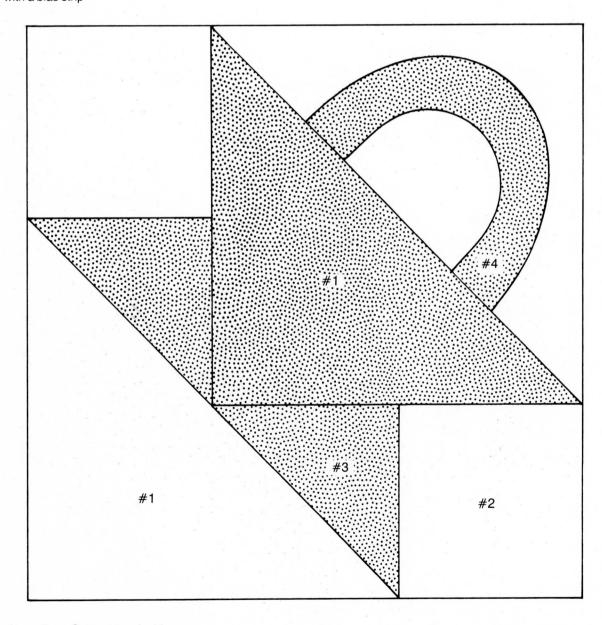

Full-size pattern. Cut apart and add seams.

Fox And Geese

One pretty color serves to hold together and brighten a scrap-bag quilt of what appears to be largely shirtings. This should be a simple enough design for a beginner, and could be pieced by machine. The blocks are almost 8½ inches on the diagonal (6 inches square), which should help you in figuring how many you need across and how many you need lengthwise. The pieced blocks alternate with colored ones, 6 inches square plus seams.

There's no border other than the pink triangles cut by halving the blocks along the edges. A plain white binding is used, or you may find a colored one more interesting and more practical.

For each pieced block cut:
2 dark #1
4 white #2
6 dark #3
10 white #3
1 colored 6-inch square block

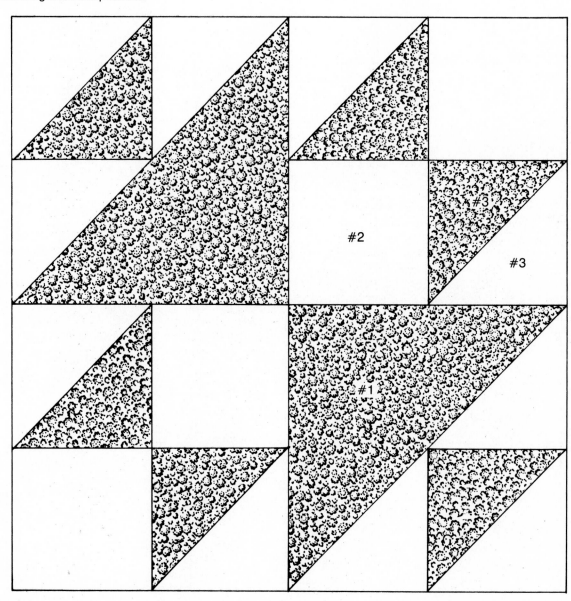

Full-size pattern. Cut apart and add seams.

Birds In Flight

Simplicity and the one little trick of using a basic print fabric for the background and lots of happy scrap-bag pieces makes this a good quilt for anyone to try, beginner or expert. The Sunburst quilting and Flying Geese border are perfect accents to the classic design.

For each block cut:
1 right-angle 9-inch triangle, add seams
6 dark #1
3 light #1

For Flying Geese border cut:
numerous scrap-bag pieces #1
twice as many background print pieces #2

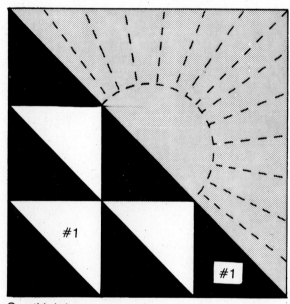

One-third size pattern.

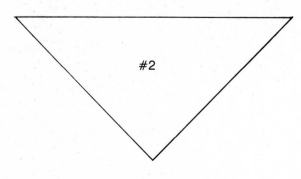

Full-size pattern. Cut apart and add seams.

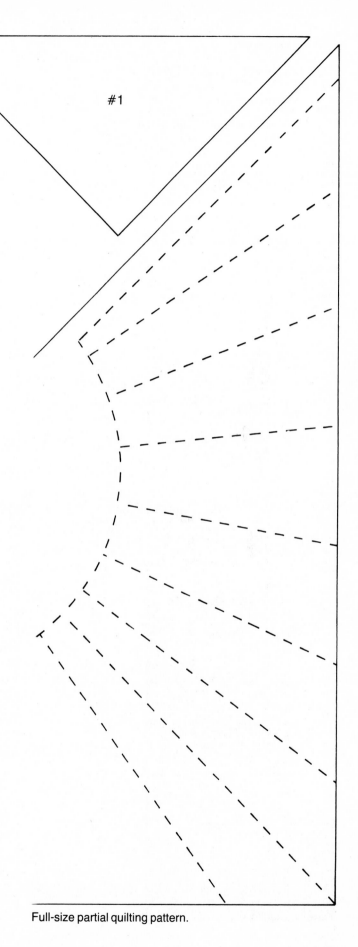

Full-size partial quilting pattern.

Streaks Of Lightning

Various patterns representing lightning have been popular from the earliest days of pieced quilts. These two patterns are on a large scale, easy to machine piece. We have added some softening touches in the two possible quilting designs. They can be used on every piece or alternated with a more rigidly geometric design.

For the brick design cut:
Equal number of half light and half dark bricks, 3¾ inches by 8 inches, add seams

For the triangle design cut:
Equal number of half light and half dark triangles, 12 inches on the right-angle side, add seams

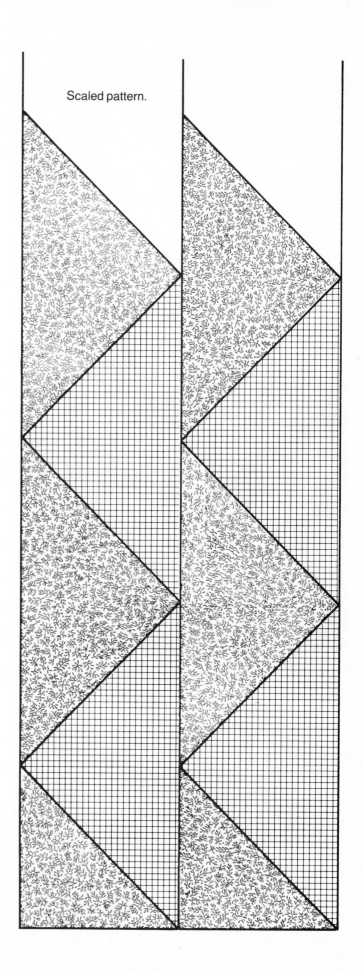

Scaled pattern.

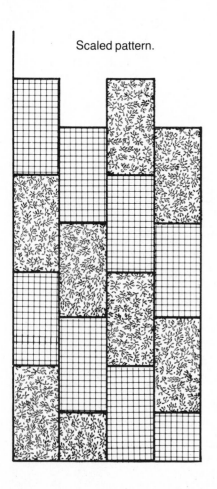

Scaled pattern.

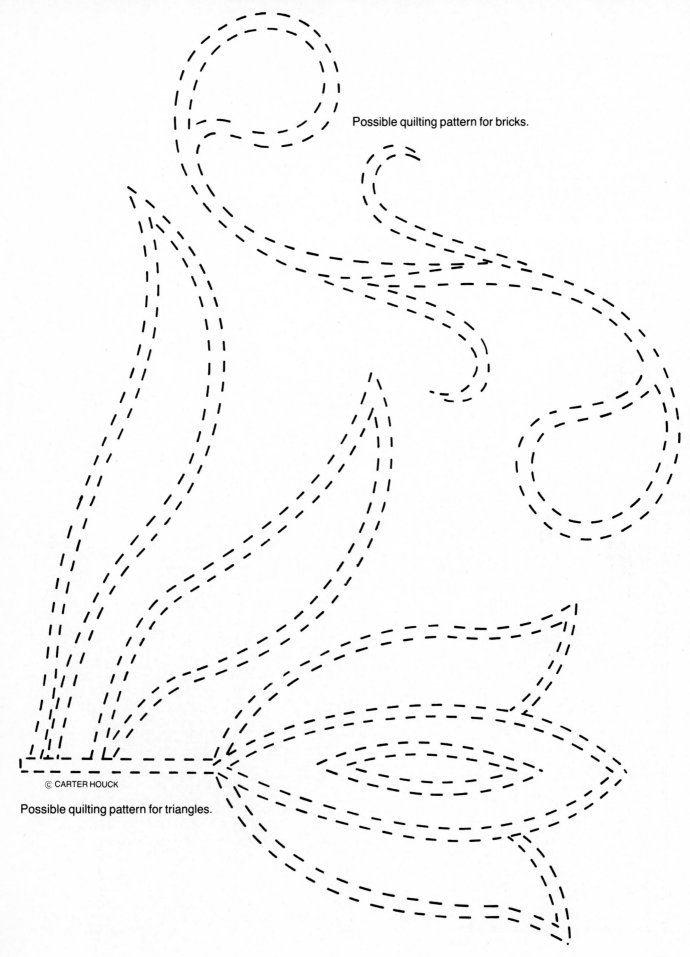

Possible quilting pattern for bricks.

© CARTER HOUCK

Possible quilting pattern for triangles.

Square Within A Square

Have you been saving old silk ties and scarves, and tiny scraps of velvet and velveteen? This dainty little design gives you an ideal opportunity to use them. You might make a small wall hanging or a large tote bag to glow and sparkle in Victorian splendor. If Victorian is not your cup of tea, tiny prints and pastels could be used for a crib quilt. Or you can enlarge the pattern for use as a full-size bed quilt.

For each pieced block cut:
    4 light #1
    4 medium or dark #2
    4 light #3
    1 dark #4
    1 medium #5

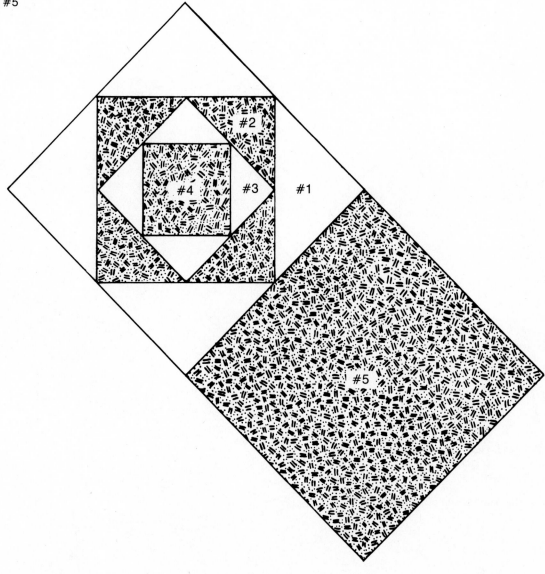

Full-size pattern. Cut apart and add seams.